Impact

A Step-by-Step Plan to Create the
World You Want to Live In

Impact

Christen Brandt and Tammy Tibbetts

PUBLICAFFAIRS

New York

PublicAffairs
Hachette Book Group
1290 Avenue of the Americas, New York, NY 10104
www.publicaffairsbooks.com
@Public_Affairs

Printed in the United States of America

First Edition: November 2020

Published by PublicAffairs, an imprint of Perseus Books, LLC, a subsidiary of Hachette Book Group, Inc. The PublicAffairs name and logo is a trademark of the Hachette Book Group.

The Hachette Speakers Bureau provides a wide range of authors for speaking events. To find out more, go to www.hachettespeakersbureau.com or call (866) 376-6591.

The publisher is not responsible for websites (or their content) that are not owned by the publisher.

Print book interior design by Amy Quinn.

Library of Congress Control Number: 2020944686

ISBNs: 978-1-5417-5678-6 (hardcover); 978-1-5417-5677-9 (ebook)

LSC-C

1 2020

To all the girls we've met on the path to our North Star,
in hopes that this will illuminate theirs

Yesterday I was clever, so I wanted to change the world.
Today I am wise, so I am changing myself.

—Rumi

CONTENTS

INTRODUCTION

WHEN YOU THINK of a changemaker, who do you picture in your mind's eye?

Perhaps you see Nelson Mandela, sowing the seeds of peace in his country. Or Malala Yousafzai, risking her life to speak out against the Taliban, or Tarana Burke, whose two simple words on social media, "me too," sparked a movement that knocked abusers out of power. Maybe you think of a leader you know in your own community. There is no shortage of inspiration.

Tell the truth, though: Do you ever picture yourself?

Most people don't, and it's time to set the record straight.

You, reader, *are* a changemaker. You are capable of enormous impact over the span of your life, whether you've already had a head start creating it or not. People often ask us how to make a difference, and we find that most underestimate their own potential. Wanting to create change doesn't automatically come with any way of knowing how to take the first steps, and it can feel like too big a task to take on by yourself.

So: What is standing in the way between who you are and the changemaker you're meant to be?

Maybe you don't know where to start. When you turn on the news, you see a mess of immigration policy, the surge of racism, and the dangers of a broken political system. Alt-right views and fake news spread on social media and have compromised democracy. The planet faces irreparable damage. You see migrant camps at borders, nationalism gaining traction, wildfires raging, women sexually abused—it can feel utterly overwhelming. It's easier to turn a blind eye in defeat, or in the hope somebody else will take care of it.

But, deep down inside, you're not the kind of person who turns away, or else you wouldn't have picked up this book. And what you're holding in your hands now *is* a starting point. Your curiosity to come on this journey has effectively begun the work that will help you turn your anger and frustration into an action plan. It will fall into place sooner than you think.

Maybe you think your efforts will be insignificant. Your small steps can seem tiny compared to large movements like Black Lives Matter, Moms Demand Action, #MeToo, or Fridays for Future. And, even when you are contributing, it can seem impossible to navigate such a complex space, where one misstep could lead to your cancelation. Suddenly, "changing the world" feels too big to take on. Is it even worth it to try?

This is a challenge we all face, and all of those people you admire started where you are today, feeling that things could be better. That it didn't have to be this way. Established changemakers didn't start with it all figured out. They started with that same feeling. Besides: Small, individual efforts give movements their power; once you learn how to link your good deeds to collective efforts, you'll see a completely different outcome.

Maybe you're not sure if it's the right time. You feel too broke, too inexperienced, or just too exhausted. Sure, you want to take on that new project, volunteer role, or leadership commitment . . . but maybe *after* work shows down, maybe once you get that new job, once you settle in after your wedding, once your kids are older . . . maybe later.

You may be skeptical of whether you can live up to another set of goals when it's hard enough to stick to a New Year's resolution. It will be very tempting to push all this down the priority list. We get it. Please note, we abide by airplane safety rules around here: Put your oxygen mask on first, because you cannot be in service to others if you're strug-gling. If you lose your job, for instance, you would understandably want to scale back on other commitments until you find a new one. If you have student loans, you want to pay those off. Fortunately, creating im-pact is a long-game approach, and the work you do to get yourself to a place where you can give back is part of the plan, too.

But, barring deep personal hardship, there are times when we all need to rearrange our priorities and set boundaries to do what matters to us. A popular mantra among entrepreneurs is "start before you're ready" because most of the time, people underestimate their potential and hold off for a "perfect time" when there never really is one. The two of us believe that by focusing your efforts, you can maximize whatever time and resources you do have. Once you begin your service, it be-comes a virtuous cycle with scientifically proven health benefits, and you'll gain the momentum to keep going. That will give you a sense of satisfaction that helps you sleep at night. Trust the process!

Or, maybe you just feel alone in making sense of your scat-tered contributions. And if that's the case, you've stumbled onto the million-dollar question: Why is it that when it comes to your legacy, your mark on the world—your *impact*—you're left to your own de-vices? No one's there to tell you how to direct your resources or to congratulate you when you're way ahead of the curve or even to re-veal whether your generosity is accidentally causing mayhem halfway around the world. How do you know if you'll leave the world better off than when you arrived?

Think of all the areas in which people seek direction from others: career, finance, relationships. Career coaches, financial advisors, and therapists are becoming more and more common for those who can afford them. It's transformational when someone fixes attention on *you*, to guide you through critical, often long-term life decisions. And if you haven't hired someone to do that, let's assume you've built support networks, found mentors, and read lots of books to figure out the best lifelong strategies. These life-changing decisions about work, money, and love seem to require a whole entourage of professional guidance, mentors, and support. Why is your impact treated differently? Why do people have to figure this out alone?

Well, not everyone does. There's one notable exception: People who have tremendous fortunes and influence—think Bill and Melinda Gates, the Obamas, Oprah Winfrey, Meghan Markle, or huge companies like Google, Starbucks, and Patagonia—rely on Impact Advisors. Impact Advisors help Impact Planners position themselves in relation to real needs in the world, by determining where they bring value. They help them develop their narratives and messaging around why they do what they do. They run risk assessments, facilitate partnerships, and define what successful outcomes look like. Sounds nice, doesn't it?

Allow us to introduce ourselves: Hi. We're Christen and Tammy. You're worthy of this guidance, too, and we're here to help. We're going to leave you with an Impact Plan that's tailored to *you*.

We believe effective changemaking skills should be accessible to anyone, and that's why we're here, ready to be your very own Impact Advisors.

As you turn the pages, we will show you, step by step, how to create a lifelong Impact Plan. An Impact Plan is your *personalized* strategy for shaping the world you want to live in. It gives you focus, purpose, and fulfillment.

We can't stress enough how important the personalized piece is. You can only change the world by first changing your own life: your habits, priorities, biases, and thoughts, for starters.

We know the power of having a focus and adapting our life to it. In our case, starting in our early twenties, we grew a multi-million-dollar nonprofit called She's the First (STF) from the ground up. STF teams up with local organizations around the globe to make sure girls are educated, respected, and heard. Ultimately, we fight for a world where every girl chooses her own future.

Christen is Chief Programs Officer and travels frequently around East and West Africa, South Asia, and Latin America, working side by side with local partners to improve programs for the most vulnerable girls. (This helps lower school dropout rates and sets girls up to break the cycle of poverty.) Tammy is Chief Executive Officer, and despite being famously shy in high school, she discovered her forte is in building community and relationships. She shows people how to contribute their most valuable assets—time, money, and talent—for the good of others.

We have more than enough inspiration and mistakes to share after mobilizing hundreds of thousands of supporters who come from many walks of life. You need not start an organization to use our techniques; to be quite frank, that's the last thing we'd recommend. The good news is, you can start small and still see rewarding results. To give you that perspective, we've hit up our network to ensure that we can offer you diverse examples of success. On the journey we're about to take together, you'll meet some of our friends and role models from around the world who have positively impacted others.

We know it can feel intimidating to think about creating change, especially when you're living under so many broken systems. But we're not focusing on overhauling the healthcare system (yet)—for now, we're just focusing on what *you* are capable of. A good Impact Plan integrates into your everyday choices, allowing you to start small and work your way up to bigger goals. Those incremental actions eventually create seismic shifts in your worldview and experience. Beyond your impact on others, with this commitment, you'll unlock the happiness, satisfaction, and joy that comes from authentically aligning your actions with your values. Your Impact Plan acknowledges your contributions aren't limited to what you directly provide. Your impact heavily leans toward what you can inspire *others* to do, and it's what you can do *with* them that will ultimately ripple out to your endgame.

We're not the kind of people who will tell you how many lives you would save if only you donated the cost of your morning latte. Good on you if that's what you choose to do, but we don't want to cut off anyone's caffeine supply (least of all our own). Creating an impact is not about what you are giving up; it's about what you gain by making smarter choices on how you spend your time, money, and talents. It's about turning up the volume on a part of your voice that had unintentionally been silent all these years.

We're writing this book because, amid all the world's drudgery, a universal truth prevails: People *want* to do good. We all want to do better. We all want to know that we're creating more positivity than chaos, that we're leaving a legacy we can be proud to call our own. That's what your Impact Plan is all about. It's how you can tackle the issues that matter most, even if you have to do it inside very broken systems. It's how you know that what you're doing matters, and how you can track your progress along the way.

Your Impact Plan is like a living, breathing plant that needs your attention to grow and thrive—and ideally, a plant you'll *want* to water. It's a one-page document that you can tape to your bedroom wall or stick on the fridge and then pull down to update from time to time. It becomes a part of your identity and what gets you out of bed in the morning. So we will also work with you to keep your momentum going, because there are people out there who need you.

WE KNEW WE HAD TO WRITE THIS BOOK after an emotional, out-of-character moment we had in front of our students. See, after nearly a decade of speaking to large groups, we thought we had our composure locked down. We have different personalities, for sure—Tammy is measured, calm, and practical in how she tackles challenges, while Christen fearlessly plunges in head first—but both of us have always been strong and steady leaders, because we had to be. We started She's the First at a young age, so we often made ourselves look tougher than we felt. We needed business executives and foundation heads to trust us, even though we might have been half their age. We needed our staff, just a handful of years younger than us, to do the same.

And yet, one evening in April 2018 we learned we are only human after all—and that leaders don't always need to be so tough.

We were in Guatemala for a week piloting a new program of She's the First called the Community Impact Fellowship. STF has more than two hundred campus chapters, or clubs, at high schools, colleges, and universities that are involved in fundraising and advocacy for girls' education and rights. The fellowship in Guatemala combined students on scholarship in Latin America and East Africa—young women who were the first in their families to attend high school—with students who were members of our American campus chapters. Each of the eleven students had created a project to support women or girls in her own community.

We gathered these young women in Antigua, Guatemala, for an intensive kickoff week. Antigua is gorgeous: Every street you walk down has vibrantly painted doorways and walls. Flowers ooze out of their pots, begging to be your next photo subject. Look up on a clear day and you'll see two volcanoes, Agua and Fuego (Water and Fire), that command your respect. It was a stunning change of scenery and a big step outside the students' comfort zones. For six days, we partnered with two dynamic facilitators, a bilingual duo who translated the workshops in Spanish *and* English the whole time. The end goal: Make sure every student left knowing how to craft her impact in the world, using her project as an actionable first step.

Throughout the week, we presented the fellows deep lessons on power, social stratification, privilege, and more, with interactive activities involving discussion, role playing, and movement. They applied these lessons to their project plans.

On the last day, the fellows got up in front of each other and delivered an impact statement: "I want to _____ because I believe that _____. Therefore, my project is _____. And I will find success when _____." Upon presenting this razor-focused, tangible plan with identifiable outcomes, each student had to stay standing and soak up a raucous applause and cheers from the group. Each and every one nailed it.

A few hours later, we all sat in a circle to close out the fellowship with final reflections. The mood had completely shifted as the group's triumphs turned into bittersweet goodbyes. Everyone would return home the next day, wherever in the world that might be. For all, home was a place where *no one* would fully understand the transformation that happened this past week, as each young woman discovered, for the first time, the impact she is truly capable of making in the world.

As we sat in the circle, a polished stone passed through our hands, giving the person holding it the opportunity to speak. On her turn, we watched each girl massage it in the palm of her hand as she gathered her thoughts.

A college student from the United States, a daughter to South Asian immigrants, clasped the stone tightly and hugged her cardigan around her as she shared a private piece of her backstory. "My parents love me but they weren't around much, working constantly, missing special moments. I've felt lonely for a lot of my life, and that continues when I'm at school and people go out to party hard and I just don't want to." She paused, then broke into a smile. "I realize now that I can create a family across borders and we can continue to be here for each other, even through WhatsApp."

Each girl told her own truth, but what they all shared was a sense that they had found their purpose, along with a new perspective. A white teen from the southern US talked about how misguided she had been, when she learned and, for a while, believed that her American education set her up to solve the complex problems of girls living abroad. This week of getting to know the other girls had helped her understand that learning was a two-way street and that her new global community could help her understand the world's challenges in new ways.

A young Indigenous woman from rural Peru crisscrossed her feet and glanced down at her sneakers before looking up to make eye contact with her new friends. She grappled to find the words to share what she felt in Spanish. A translator softly echoed her words in English: "Before this week, I had never left my country. Where I'm from, everyone is struggling so much to live day by day; there is no chance to think about helping others. But that is what I have wanted to do. No one in my class understands me. This is the first time I found friends who share my goals."

And this is when we lost it. We broke our own rule to never cry in public, no matter how difficult our work became. Tears quietly streamed down Tammy's cheeks, and Christen handed her a tissue and squeezed her hand. When it was Christen's turn to talk, she erupted like Fuego into an ugly cry. Polished and professional went right out the window.

This moment reminded us how safe and empowering spaces carved out for girls and women can be a haven away from the impossible difficulties of real life, poverty, discrimination, or violence at home. In these spaces, no one is exercising their power over you, so you no longer need the defense mechanisms you've built up by living in a society that is constantly working to hold you down. These spaces allow us to connect with our deepest selves, with our *why*, and with others who share it.

In circles like this one, we all find what binds us together. The students found what bound them to one another was a power to impact their communities and a deep desire to rewrite the story of what it means to be a girl. In one week, they had been immersed in a new way of seeing their role in the world. There was no going back.

As for us, we drew deep connections between the students and our younger selves. Of course, many times before we had seen the impact of programs She's the First funded. This was the first time, though, that we led a program investing in young women's own changemaking ideas, and that was electrifying.

We have no regrets about our tears now—that vulnerability unlocked our strength and led us to ask ourselves after the retreat, *How can we replicate this experience in a way that anyone, anywhere could access? How can we expand the circle?* And then it clicked.

What you're holding is the answer.

In this book, we guide you through your own process of identifying the outcome you want to see in the world and how to play your part in getting there. And just as the fellows wished for, we'll furnish you with the tools to build a like-minded support network around you. We've created several exercises for you to complete along the way. We recommend turning a new notebook into your Impact Journal. You can also gather with friends, a book club, or a partner to talk through the steps. You might find it helpful to read through everything once and then go back and do the exercises with intention, giving each the time you need to do it well. After you finish the exercises in Part I, you may feel ready to take on the world, but stick with us for the chapters that follow. We'll make sure you've got the proper techniques and perspectives to evaluate your work, avoiding some pitfalls that befell us and others who came before you.

You may already sense that deep changemaking is not for the faint of heart. You start with small, easy steps, and when you go all in, it can be messy and draining for a good stretch of the climb before you reach peaks of achievement. But we believe anyone can do it. The least we could do is spare you some dead ends and rocky roads, or just help make them a lot less bumpy, by sharing what we've learned through a decade of entrepreneurship. This is no kumbaya book, contrary to the campfire-like bonding moment that inspired it. We left our pom-poms at home. We had to make room for the brutal honesty, vulnerability, clarity, and occasional embarrassing stories we've pulled from our experiences. All you need to bring is an open mind; we'll make sure you walk away with a new set of goggles through which to view the world. You'll be able to use that vision to unearth your passion and:

- Create a concrete plan for generating a sustained impact in one area, which you can put into action immediately
- Build a practical and progressive understanding of what it really means to "change the world" so you're not accidentally contributing to the problems you want to solve
- Learn candid and untold lessons from the two of us and others to pull you through the tough moments
- Gather the tools that will help you stay on track to live a purposeful life you're proud of

By the end of this book, you'll be claiming the title of changemaker and getting your friends to sign on too. Let's do this!

Part I

THE PLAN

chapter one

FINDING YOUR NORTH STAR

> I read of a man who stood to speak at the funeral
> of a friend. He referred to the dates on the
> tombstone from the beginning . . . to the end.
> He noted that first came the date of birth and spoke
> of the following date with tears, but he said what
> mattered most of all was the dash between those years.
>
> —Linda Ellis

BELIEVE IT OR not, a punctuation mark compelled you to pick up this book. And it's not a question mark, despite all the answers you're searching for here.

It's a dash.

Specifically, it's *your* dash, the one that separates the day you were born from the day you will die. Yes, we'll be the first to admit that sounds a bit morbid . . . and also deeply meaningful. This little punctuation mark packs so much power, it should get you thinking: *What will my dash mean for the world?*

When you're contributing to the greater good of humanity and you feel a spark inside, that's a hint about your dash. The moments when you're volunteering, working to elect a capable leader, or protecting the planet for all the little kids who will inherit it—just to name a few examples—are chances to express your dash while you're alive and well. You, like both of us, want to know that the world is just a tiny bit better because you live in it.

Even though you've already done *some* good, you want your life to mean something. You suspect that there is untapped potential inside you. You know you have skills and ideas to contribute to movements, and perhaps you're just not sure how to apply them without rocking the boat and throwing your other responsibilities in life overboard—or where to focus when you care about so damn much.

In practical terms, you have many options from here: Should you take that next promotion or change careers entirely? Should you save up and work hard to donate more later? Should you stash your stuff in storage and head off on a worldwide volunteering voyage? Should you go all in with a local community project or invest in global causes? Should you run for office or launch an advocacy project?

These question marks (our other favorite piece of punctuation, obviously) are part of the journey that gives our lives purpose, beyond our friendships and family relationships or faith. Perhaps you're looking for that extra bit of self-actualization outside of your home, in a way that previous generations of your family didn't think about because they were focused on setting you up for a better life. Nailing down that larger purpose often fluctuates somewhere between "changing the world," which feels too big to take on, and "doing good," which feels too vague, gentle, and earnest.

This is why we developed the framework we call the Impact Plan. We want to help you make this journey more manageable without diluting its importance. Impact is a deeply personal process, beginning with an examination of your own story; continuing with an understanding of your resources, priorities, and biases; and ending with new commitments to action.

We tested the Impact Plan in workshops with professionals in their twenties and thirties. The first questions we asked them were: *Why?*

Why do you want to take this workshop? Why do you feel you need an Impact Advisor? The answers inevitably were:

> "I feel I'm not giving back enough and I want to help make change."
>
> "While I do various forms of volunteering activities, I know there is more that I can do and that needs to be done . . . and I don't have any idea how to be structured about this!"
>
> "I feel like since I've joined 'corporate America' I've stopped giving back—and I'd love to add value again."
>
> "I have a vision, but I don't know how to get there. How does my plan bloom?"

You might sense a theme emerging. Many, many people have the drive to create change. The gratification of doing so is real, if not addictive. However, it's also fleeting. Where to start becomes such a large hurdle that people end up giving in sporadic ways, volunteering once per year, donating to friends' birthday fundraisers, chipping in to a political campaign—it never quite feels like it all adds up. With only so much time and so many resources, we each need a sustainable way to commit long enough to see the real dent we're making in an issue. Missing from common wisdom on how to create impact was a strategy on how to integrate it into everyday life. Without that, what's the point?

As your Impact Advisors, our part of the bargain is making sure you have a solid plan to create tangible, sustainable impact, now and into the future. Your part? Being open to the exercises and reflection opportunities, which have corresponding worksheets wherever you see a ✳. You can easily revisit these exercises whenever your plan needs a tune-up.

OUR FIRST STEP IS PINPOINTING YOUR NORTH STAR. You've probably heard of a North Star as a way of talking about your purpose. Your North Star is what you want your dash to stand for. It lights you up and guides you in making the most fulfilling life decisions, much like how, before Google Maps, our forebears used the brightest stars in the sky to find their way. Our definition of a North Star connects your actions with *vision*.

In your Impact Plan, the North Star represents your end goal, the future you want to see. Like real stars that are trillions of miles away, a North Star can feel distant from the world you live in today. That's okay. The point is that your North Star is something you can *visualize*. When you're describing *a future world where* _____, your North Star is what you fill in that blank with. Perhaps it is a future of racial justice, gender equality, religious tolerance, financial freedom, universal education, or environmental sustainability. Your vision could be at any scale—focused on your local community all the way up to the planet at large.

When there is so much to care about, your North Star helps you filter out the opportunities that do not match your desired focus so you aren't overspending energy elsewhere. When you are overwhelmed, your North Star keeps you inspired, grounded, and hopeful for what could be.

For some people, choosing a North Star feels paralyzing. If this is you, don't worry; we'll come back to that challenge and get you unstuck. First, let's look at some people who are so sure of their North Star that it's as if it's written in stone. That's actually how one woman we admire, Tiffany Dufu, thinks of it. Tiffany is the founder of The Cru, a peer coaching company for women. Long before she made that entrepreneurial leap, she held fundraising positions at nonprofits and schools serving girls, served on the board of directors for Girls Who Code, and authored a book called *Drop the Ball* to help women cultivate the skill of letting go. She frequently talks on stage about the nine words that will be on her tombstone one day (right under her dash): "She got to as many women as she could." Tiffany is driven by advancing women and girls, and when you look at her career and the work she's committed herself to, that's the through line.

Her rock-solid conviction surprises some people: How does she know this is her calling? It's a lot of pressure to choose the *one outcome* you want to orient your life around when there seems to be one injustice, one marginalized group, one natural disaster after another calling for your attention. Tiffany sums up her approach in a simple motto: "Purpose is simply commitment inspired by experience."

In other words, commit to a North Star that's informed by your experience. Use Tiffany's advice to whittle down your focus, or to solidify it, so you come out of this chapter with a clear narrative on what matters to you and *why*. Draw on the life experiences that define who you are today.

If you've had positive moments of gratitude, support, and strength, these advantages make you who you are, and they inform how you want to pay it forward. Or maybe there was a time when you had extreme anxiety, felt completely overwhelmed and saddened. What was happening in your life when you felt that way? If you experienced poverty, racism, bullying, cyber harassment, abuse, or any difficult circumstances unique to you . . . those negative experiences you've accumulated can push you, too.

Jamira Burley is an unforgettable example of someone who found a bright North Star in the darkness of tragedy and hardship. Jamira is the first of sixteen siblings to graduate from high school in Philadelphia. Both of her parents and twelve of her thirteen brothers have been incarcerated. She's lost several relatives to gun violence, including her brother who was murdered when she was fifteen. "I believe you should be the expert of your own experience," Jamira says, and for her, that means speaking up on issues she is, or was, personally affected by and feeling qualified to effect change in those areas.

Even as a teenager, Jamira would not wait for someone with fancy credentials to come along and fix the problems in her community. After her brother's death, she organized an antiviolence program in her high school—and it ended up reducing the rate of violence by 30 percent. The governor then provided funding for the program's implementation at ten high schools in the city.

You rarely realize as a child how tied your personal experience is to the larger forces of policy, law, or discrimination. Systemic inequalities are the unequal outcomes built into our institutions. As Jamira got older and became the first in her family to attend university, she recognized that a lack of access to quality education was a root cause for the violence she grew up around.

The issues of gun violence prevention and education ended up intertwining and feeding into her ultimate outcome—a world where young people reach their potential. As an activist and Impact Advisor herself, Jamira's North Star guides her to create pathways for youth to escape the environments they didn't choose to be born into and then to go back to change their communities. Now in her thirties, Jamira has the credentials of working for the mayor of Philadelphia, Amnesty International USA, Hillary Clinton's presidential campaign, and the Global Business Coalition for Education. She was also named a White House Champion of Change during the Obama administration. And yet, despite all these amazing accomplishments on her résumé, Jamira would tell you what most qualifies her as a changemaker is not where she has worked, but what she lived through in West Philadelphia.

Christen's North Star: Women and Girls are Safe and Able to Thrive

When I was born, my mom was nineteen, graduated from high school, and unsure of what would come next. My father was also nineteen, and a casual drug dealer, so my mom felt pretty confident that he shouldn't be in whatever future was in store for the two of us. I grew up in a full house with my mom, my grandparents, and three of my mom's younger sisters. I remember sneaking into one aunt's closet to try on her sequined prom dress, and another aunt feeding me icing sandwiches, with cake frosting and sprinkles smeared between the folded sides of a slice of white bread. I was surrounded by women and happy about it. But there was a consistent theme in my childhood: The men who surrounded my mom and aunts . . . they weren't always great. My mom, my aunts, my grandma all shared a mantra: *Don't trust men.*

When I was six or seven, I happily climbed into the car with an aunt to pick up her kids for the weekend. In the parking lot where we were supposed to meet her ex-husband, my aunt got out of the car. I stayed inside, watching cars drive past, as the minutes stretched on and on. Eventually, my aunt made it back to the car, crying, barely breathing, red in the face and shaking as she apologized, frantically turning the ignition over and over, willing the car to start faster. He had been angry she was late; he refused to give her the kids, and, when she argued, he became physical with her.

When I was ten, we moved in with my brother's father, a man of few words, almost none of them kind. We couldn't watch TV when he wanted to. Talking at the dinner table resulted in being sharply and quickly criticized or worse, so we generally kept quiet. Holidays and birthdays became an exercise in trying to fit the joy around the edges of what he allowed us to do. I thought it was normal. Growing up, I remember joking that my stepdad was such a grouch, but I said I could tell he liked me, because sometimes he would tease me or he would change the oil in my car without saying anything to me.

All along the way, the women in my life repeated their favorite mantra: *You can't trust men. You can't trust men. You can't trust men.* And all the while, they worked, they organized parties for one another, they supported one another, they crafted happy moments for all of us.

So I pushed down those memories of why "you can't trust men" for a long time in favor of my memories of how women are strong. I vowed to work for girls and women, first as a magazine editor, then full-time at She's the First. I became a self-defense instructor for survivors of violence and went viral for a post about catcalling. And still, I didn't connect my negative experiences to what I was fighting for.

That happened years later, in my late twenties, in the car with my mom and stepdad on Christmas Day, traveling to an aunt's house for

(continues)

dinner. My mom and I were discussing the Band Aid song "Do They Know It's Christmas?" You know the one: They talk about Africa as a place of no snow, where nothing grows, in an attempt to raise money for a famine. We were bantering back and forth about how much money the song raised, and how ultimately terrible it was, and my stepdad, who had been in a foul mood all day, suddenly exploded. Sitting choked with fear and tears in the back seat of a car as a twenty-seven-year-old while a grown man screams at you for a difference in opinion, or because he's simply grown tired of hearing you talk, is one of those life-defining moments that split your life into a *before* and an *after*.

Before, I was drawn to working with and for women and girls because of the strength of the women who shaped my life and the potential I saw in girls.

After, I was drawn to working with and for women and girls because of the strength and potential I saw there—*and* because I could finally see that a system of oppressive patriarchy had directly shaped my own life.

It can take a long time to realize that what's normal for you shouldn't be normal for anyone. But it's those realizations that often shape our vision for the world we want to live in. I want a better world for girls, yes, and I want every girl to have a quality education—but more than anything, I never want a girl to sit in the back seat of a car crying and choked by fear, no matter her age. I want a world where men are no longer empowered or encouraged to rule through fear. No one should be able to take away your voice, your agency, or your choices.

Tammy's North Star: Girls and Women Have the Opportunities and Resources to Achieve Their Dreams

When I was younger, I was *excruciatingly* shy and often stood in my own way because of low self-esteem. I remember being sick to my stomach before giving a presentation, and I was such a social outsider that teachers would pull me aside to ask if I was okay.

I know that this is a barrier that pales in comparison to institutional injustice that others face, and that I benefited from the privileges of my race as well as the hard work and sacrifices earlier generations of my working-class family made for me. I grew up in a stable, loving, two-parent home in a safe suburb with quality public schools. But low self-esteem can impact any girl, regardless of her background, and the messaging she sees in the world makes it infinitely worse. It felt insurmountable to me.

When senior year of high school rolled around, it was time for the long-standing tradition of doling out superlatives to the graduating class: Most Likely to Change the World, Most Likely to Be President, Best Smile, and so on. I received one of the less desirable superlatives in the book—Most Shy. For the yearbook, the photographer asked me to stand behind a pillar and peek my head out, as if I was scared and hiding. As if I didn't want to take up space. That was nearly twenty years ago and, still, I remember it, down to the striped turtleneck sweater I was wearing, like it was yesterday. That day was the turning point. I vowed to myself that I was going to prove this superlative wrong.

I was about to be the first woman in my family to pursue a bachelor's degree and choose a profession that was also a passion. So, in college, I resolved to start fresh and make use of my voice—as a writer and active classroom participant—and I did! I wanted to take up space so that I could make space for others. My calling became more powerful than the shyness.

After I graduated, I landed my dream job at *Seventeen*, where I could be part of an editorial team making millions of readers feel more confident every day. When I was seventeen, I had never fathomed I could work for the magazine I didn't even feel "cool enough" to read at that age or run a multi-million-dollar organization or be an author . . . but with my education and unconditional love and support from my parents, it was possible.

(continues)

Now that I'm in my thirties and married, I often reflect on how different my path was from that of previous generations. My great-grandmother had her first child when she was seventeen. Her third daughter, my grandmother, would get married when she was not much older than that, and in her wedding announcement from 1948, she would be introduced to the world only as "Mrs." in front of her husband's full name. She was just "the bride." Other than descriptions of her wedding dress, she was noted as a high school graduate and that was it. When my mom was married, she didn't get to choose where the ceremony would be or have it be as intimate as she wanted.

In 2018, seventy years after my grandmother's wedding, I got married. I didn't have a wedding announcement, but I published an article called "How to Have a Feminist Wedding." I wrote about how my husband and I decided to commemorate our marriage as an equal partnership. This is just one of many examples I could give that show the change that is possible in a generation or two. I had the chance to control my future and my narrative in ways my great-grandmother, grandmother, and mother never did. Higher education and my mom's commitment to breaking that cycle with her children gave me an unprecedented opportunity.

I am not Mrs. anyone. I am not Most Shy. I am whoever I want to be and I navigate the world as I choose. This feels like a luxury and yet it should be a basic right. And that's where my North Star comes from. I envision a world where every girl and woman has the chance to write her own story.

Examining your own life as inspiration for your North Star makes you an authentic and compassionate advocate and ally. It's your *why*. A connection to your personal history is what keeps you humble, passionate, and most effective.

Author, physician, and professor Rachel Naomi Remen has struggled with Crohn's disease her entire life, which has informed her view of life and medicine. She wrote a piece that illuminated the difference between "helping," "fixing," and "serving" that is popular among non-profit workers. It's one of the reasons we push you to see your North Star as self-sustaining, to avoid the word *help* in how you approach the change you want to create. Remen says when you help, you see life as weak. When you fix, you see life as broken. And when you serve, you see life as whole. "Fixing and helping may be the work of the ego," she writes, "and service the work of the soul. . . . Fixing and helping create a distance between people, but we cannot serve at a distance. We can only serve that to which we are profoundly connected."

Think about how powerful that empathy is. The context of how you experience an issue may differ greatly from how others do, based on privilege, geography, and what makes you unique, but that doesn't stop you from relating to them. For example, we are both first-generation college graduates. We understand what it means to use our education to unlock levels of social mobility that previous generations of our family didn't have. These pieces of our identity drew us to be passionate about fighting for equality alongside girls who are first in their families to graduate from high school and create new paths. That said, we have limitations in understanding the experience of girls who are facing dangers and instability we never had to think about.

Gaps between your frame of reference and others' simply means it's critical to have ongoing conversations in which you listen more than you speak. Focus on learning more about the issue you're fighting and the people affected by it to avoid projecting your own experience . . . and there's a whole lot more where that came from in Part II of this book.

After reading these examples, it's your turn. If you had to pick the top experiences or circumstances that make you who you are today, what would they be? As you read through this next section, use the workbook or your Impact Journal to jot down your thoughts. ❋1

WHAT MOVES YOU?

In case unpacking your life story doesn't bring you immediate clarity on your North Star, here's another tactic to identify it. If you were to pop open the *New York Times* right now, what headlines would you want to click on? Notice the stories that stir emotions like anger, heartbreak, and hope. Is there a documentary you saw and can't get out of your mind? Or a nonfiction book that you couldn't keep to yourself and recommended to multiple people? An article you posted to Facebook?

Anger united the two of us on our changemaking journey. Our collaboration traces back to a news article that Tammy posted on Facebook in 2009. It was from a Liberian news outlet and shamed young women for teen pregnancies. Tammy was livid that the story failed to mention the lack of sex education provided to girls (and boys). The community had failed these girls, not the other way around. Tammy posted to Facebook that she wanted to start a social media campaign to promote the importance of girls' education. When she asked if anyone would like to join her, Christen—someone she had only met once before "in real life"—messaged her directly to express her shared anger and to jump on board . . . the rest is history.

Thinking about what pushes your buttons is a reminder that, contrary to how it sounds, a North Star isn't whimsical; it's powerful. And when you see something that threatens it, you have a visceral reaction.

Another way to locate your North Star is to think about where you spend your time. That might be in a rally, march, community service, family care, event, or volunteer or pro bono capacity.

For model Imaan Hammam, she found clues to her North Star in an unexpected place: her Instagram. "I hear from young girls on Instagram daily who look up to me as a role model," she says. Imaan spent more and more time responding to their comments and DMs while on photo shoot breaks and airport layovers. "I knew I wanted to give back to a cause that would change the lives of young girls," Imaan told us. "And since I am half Egyptian, half Moroccan, I wanted to not just help girls in the United States, where I live, but around the world. You can only give of yourself when you really believe in the cause." In her first year as an ambassador, Imaan raised more than $40,000 for girls globally through She's the First and spoke about her work at publicity events, in magazines, and on social media.

And how about where you donate? Think about the causes or situations that compel you to give, even in small amounts, to nonprofits, individuals, political campaigns, or neighborhood needs.

When you consider where you've shown up, what outcome are those groups and activities supporting? For the stories that anger you, what right or kind of person are they threatening? Now, in your Impact Journal, go back to that list of experiences that shaped you and see if you can connect them to the issues you already support and read about. Where you see overlap is the zone where you find your North Star.

WHAT YOU "SHOULD" DO

By now, you may already lean toward what could be your North Star (but if not, don't sweat it!). It's at this stage that self-doubt and second-guessing tend to emerge in our Impact Planners. There's a common sticking point: the notion of where you *should* focus to maximize impact versus what lights you up. The dreaded "should" might come from an opinionated passerby or from academics who have data-driven arguments, and it can make you feel like what you're passionate about isn't enough.

One of our Impact Planners, Raquel, struggled at first in naming her North Star. She's passionate about animal rights. It's not unusual for her to be running late because she saved an abandoned dog or because a neighbor found a stray and then brought it to Raquel, trusting she'd know what to do. At any given time, she's fostering dogs or cats, with the goal of having her own rescue one day. Raquel finds herself torn about where to focus her impact efforts. "I feel like there are so many people who need help. Should I put more time into that? Is me focusing on animals neglecting people that I could help?"

You might feel like this, too. Perhaps your passions point you toward supporting the arts as your focus, but the news keeps reminding you about *all* the issues affecting the world right now. Maybe international issues draw you in, even though you know there are families struggling on the same block where you live. These dichotomies we create in our heads are not productive, so be careful you don't get lost down this rabbit hole. When we pit worthy issues against each other, we let other people's judgment, or at least the fear of it, stand in our way. There are nearly eight billion people on this planet; no one—yourself included—can put the weight of solving *everything* on your shoulders. Not to mention, each of us has unique skills and abilities that make *more* of a difference in certain areas than in others. The purpose of an Impact Plan is to concentrate your resources behind an area of need that matches your interests and talents, not to account for all of them.

One of Tammy's first memories of volunteering in New York City was when, at age twenty-two, with zero experience, she was given the task of producing a gala. The foundation she volunteered for held their events at the fancy Four Seasons hotel. On the night of the fundraiser, Tammy remembers scrambling before doors opened, setting up the photo backdrop and registration tables, when a guest of the hotel interrupted her. She asked what the event was for. Tammy paused to explain the mission of the organization, which was to support struggling children in postwar Liberia. Her passion was met with a scowl. The woman clutched her purse a little tighter and said, "Well, you should do something for the kids *here*. There are plenty who need help." Cue Tammy's blood pressure levels rising. Stunned and unsure of how to reply, she just forced a smile and went back to multitasking.

How many times have you heard those words: "You should . . ."? They're the kiss of death for constructive conversation and collaboration. Imagine: You just launched a neighborhood bakery selling delicious pastries and coffee. And someone walks in and says, "You know, you should really think about selling plants instead!" Don't let these kinds of "you shoulds" derail you. They often come from the cheap seats, where the people who aren't taking action sit. Just as is true for any company or organization, consider expanding your work only when it aligns with your overarching goals—not because others think you should. And to those giving directives, we've since found a confident, encouraging reply suffices: "I think [insert what they think you should do] is an important need and I support your efforts. What I'm most passionate about now is [your issue or North Star of choice]."

Another way you may face this is from those "but what about . . ." questions. We heard more than once after describing She's the First: "What about the boys?" These days, we no longer feel the need to defend the reasons we personally or organizationally focus on girls—our time is better spent elsewhere. Instead, we respond with curiosity, encouragement, and our most acceptable use of "you should." We reply, "Tell me about *your* idea. You should do that!"

FOLLOWING YOUR HEART

Civil rights leader Howard Thurman famously advised: "Don't ask what the world needs. Ask what makes you come alive, and go do it. Because what the world needs is people who have come alive." We agree. We'll spend a lot of time exploring what makes you tick, because that's crucial to finding your place in the impact landscape.

There's a Japanese concept called *ikigai* that, roughly translated, means "the reason you get up in the morning." A Westernized image of *ikigai* has come to represent that sweet spot where what you're good at, what you love, what the world needs, and what you can get paid for all come together to create a balanced, fulfilled life. You'll notice that the individual's tastes and strengths—what you love and where your skills are—play a huge role. Throughout this book, keep this concept of overlap in mind. Impact doesn't just come from reacting to the world around you; it originates from your passions and strengths, too.

Keiko Feldman, an Emmy award–winning producer and a strong believer in *ikigai*, believes that you need to make an impact where you are best qualified. Her son came out in high school, and she worried about how the process would affect him. She shared her hopes and fears with a close friend, Morgan Walsh, whose own elementary-aged son had expressed a sense of gender fluidity the year before. When Morgan decided she wanted to disseminate inclusive books to libraries in their community, Keiko was the first person she called. From there, they founded Gender Nation to validate children through access to uplifting, inclusive stories that show the full spectrum of sexuality and gender identity. The two women now raise funds to ensure that inclusive

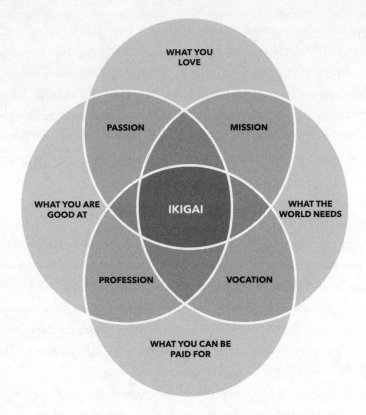

books are on the shelves at public school libraries across California (and within a few years, the nation). "I value other issues," Keiko says, "but I don't think I have the credibility or connection that makes people buy in to what I'm doing when it comes to other areas of impact. But with Gender Nation, I do. I have a kid who had to fight for who he is, who wasn't getting a message of love from other places. *That* story I am qualified to talk about."

This is why the power of your personal experience can be so critical to the area of impact where you focus. Even when running her own company full-time, Keiko makes room for Gender Nation because she knows it is where *she* can be most useful to the world. She says: "I'm in a good position to talk to donors and schools about taking these books. When you find yourself in a position to make a change, and to do it in an area you care about, you should. I can't say this is the *most* important thing in the world, but it's the thing I uniquely can do."

Speaking of "the most important" causes, who decides that anyway? Moral debates circle around where to focus and which interventions pass a certain kind of high-impact test. Welcome to the world of effective altruism, which is an evidence-based approach to philanthropy that aims to do the most good for the most lives (animal welfare included). Effective altruism prioritizes causes that have a large scale (affect many people's lives), are highly neglected (because few other people focus on them), and are highly solvable (read: cheap).

Effective altruism has both its merits and limitations. One of its strengths is a generous approach to international issues. A US dollar can indeed stretch further in other parts of the world; this is why we started She's the First with a global focus, because the few hundreds of dollars we could raise with our friends when we were younger would put a girl through her entire school year. That same amount of money would not put a dent in an American student's scholarship needs. This is one reason why we, too, recommend earmarking some of your donations for global causes (we leave how much up to you).

Another strength of effective altruism is a focus on outcomes, which we'll talk about more later, because outcomes—the results of an organization's work—are the best way to evaluate an organization. However, it is not feasible to measure all outcomes in a technical way, such as with randomized controlled trials; often, qualitative evidence and basic tracking have to suffice.

The limitations to effective altruism become more apparent when we talk about Systems Solutions, an aspect of changemaking we dive into more in Part II. For example, the charity effectiveness evaluator GiveWell, which adheres to effective altruism principles, considers one such systemic solution, education in low-income countries, to have "limited evidence of effectiveness to date." Really? You will find mountains of evidence that show otherwise from any successful education-focused nonprofit. There is a lack of funding for research in this area, however, and that's why GiveWell admits, "The evidence that education increases earnings is currently thin, and we hope that there will be more experimental studies evaluating this relationship in the future. We are also uncertain about how much value to place on social effects of education, such as reductions in fertility and marriage of young women: Our cost-effectiveness analysis relies on highly subjective value judgments which we may change our mind on in the future."

Yikes. Personally, we don't think concepts like lower rates of domestic violence or increased economic power should count as subjective, even if they are more difficult (and therefore costly) to measure. Investing in social programs is not as cheap as $5 a day for an insecticide-treated malaria net that prevents a child's death, nor as simple of an equation. After all, social change is not transactional. It's systemic. Whereas each malaria net can save a life, a book does not teach a child to read (nor does building a school), and yet, where would we be without books and schools?

The bottom line here is to be wary of weighing causes and beneficiaries against one another; it's a doomed debate. Although we encourage vetting what you get involved in through third parties familiar with the space, avoid looking for external validation of the most "moral" or important focus. Find what makes you come alive, as Thurman said, because you'll be more likely to stay committed. And that's what our Impact Planner Raquel ultimately did; she settled on the North Star that was true and invigorating to her: humane treatment for all animals.

FAST-FORWARD TO THE FUTURE

We've established that the North Star of your Impact Plan represents a vision you have for the world, and your purpose feeds into it. When you resolve the issues that rattle you, the North Star is the outcome.

In the nonprofit world, we use a term to talk about creating impact in the long run: a *theory of change*. It's one framework that allows us to look past what an organization is currently doing in order to see what needs to be done. It starts with the end goal—the long-term change you want to see. If you start with the ending you want, you can work backward, eventually arriving at the everyday actions or activities you can be doing to directly impact your end goal. Impact Plans are inspired by this concept.

Now is the perfect time for a visioning exercise based on the themes that are already emerging for your North Star. We know, we know. It sounds cheesy. But before you roll your eyes, we've seen time and again how effective it is, so we insist!

Envision this: You've just woken up, and it's twenty years in the future. You wake with a certainty that all is well in the world, that all is at peace. You know that as you progress through your day, you'll see examples of exactly that. So you go outside into your neighborhood. What do you see there? Who do you talk to? What is different about the way you interact with people or the way they interact with each other? What is different about your surroundings? What is it like when you go to work? When you turn on the news, what story is on?

Pause to close your eyes and let these scenes play out like a movie in your head. Set your phone timer for three minutes and just see what shows on the screens of your eyelids. When you're done, add any additional detail to your notes.

What does the story you've just played in your mind tell you about the changes you want to see happen between now and then? What is the overarching theme of those changes? *That* is your North Star.

Don't be afraid to be audacious; this is a broad goal that you share with millions of people, so you won't be alone in achieving it. Your North Star is your motivation. It's important that it speaks to the future you believe in, using words that light you up, almost like poetry.

We're not asking you to tattoo your North Star on your body, so your word choice doesn't have to be perfect. Keep in mind there is room to update it as you go along. For example, a decade ago, we would have told you our organization's North Star was a world where every girl reached graduation. We still champion graduation for girls, but it's not our finish line anymore. It's just a pit stop. We didn't start out with the grand plan of building a nonprofit organization that works to make sure girls everywhere are educated, respected, and heard. At first, we simply focused on funding one scholarship for one girl at a time. Our North Star was a smaller version of what it is today.

A decade ago, we committed to doing *one thing* each day that would support She's the First (in addition to working our full-time jobs in the magazine industry). It was just a social media campaign, at that point, to publicize the significance of supporting a girl who would be first in her family to graduate high school. One day the commitment may have been to email a celebrity and ask them to share our video. Another day, it was to design an info sheet that would make it easier to get press coverage. The next, it was to write up a plan for a fundraiser that would fund one year of school for one girl. The steps were *small* and the vision had a specific horizon—the day she received her high school diploma.

But a handful of years later, as we got deeper into the work, we began asking ourselves different questions. What if a girl never learned how to stand up for herself at home and ended up being pressured into an early marriage, despite her diploma? What if that marriage led her to get pregnant before she had a chance to get a job that would help her achieve financial freedom? What if she wanted to focus her time on learning a trade, rather than studying for university? Shouldn't it be her choice? We learned new lessons, and so our goals got deeper, too. What we realized was that we really envisioned a world where girls could choose their own futures.

Deepening focus doesn't just apply to organizational leadership. You'll recall Jamira Burley also updated her focus along the way, starting out with actions geared toward gun violence prevention, then integrating that focus with education, and ultimately finding youth empowerment to be the overarching theme of her impact journey. It's natural for your goals to evolve, because experience informs growth. Knowing you have that flexibility, pick a direction to get started.

To recap, here are a few tips to keep in mind in the first iteration of your North Star:

- You connect to it personally.
- It inspires you when you hear it.

- It identifies the *who*—who or what will be impacted? Ideally, the *who* is a group you identify with in some way. It can be broad: "non-binary people globally," or narrow: "elderly people in my community."
- The outcome is ultimately self-sustaining, not tasked to you or dependent on your actions.
- Avoid the verb *help* (i.e., rather than "help immigrants have equal rights," "immigrants have equal rights"). Take yourself out of the equation when you frame it.

We'll give you some general examples:

- Marginalized communities have strong mental health services
- Immigrants experience equal rights
- Justice for Indigenous communities
- Pregnancy and childbirth are safe for every mother
- The planet is protected for future generations
- People with disabilities are represented as strong and valued
- Teen girls have body acceptance role models
- Elderly adults are cared for with dignity
- Gender equality exists in the workplace
- My government thrives on diverse (gender, race, class) representation
- No one lives in fear of gun violence
- Kids in my community are healthy and educated
- Everyone in my community has a home
- All kids can explore their imagination and enjoy the arts
- Animals are treated with respect and kindness
- Extreme poverty no longer exists

(continues)

We mentioned your North Star can be like poetry, articulated in a way that lights you up. These are actual North Stars from leaders we admire:

A world where . . .

- every child has access to the knowledge and opportunities they need to achieve their full potential
    - Hamza Arsbi, founder of MindLab
- trans people have full rights and protections, empowering us to live our lives as boldly or ordinarily as we choose
    - Jackson Bird, author and digital creator
- women and girls are respected, safe, and free to express themselves fully
    - Monique Coleman, actress and activist
- every girl is able to live her brave, not perfect life
    - Reshma Saujani, founder of Girls Who Code and author of *Brave, Not Perfect*
- we center and honor the unique experiences of women of color
    - Meena Harris, founder and CEO of the Phenomenal Woman Action Campaign and author of *Kamala and Maya's Big Idea*
- no one in our communities lacks the food and nutrition they need for a healthy life
    - Adam Lowy, founder of Move for Hunger
- doors are always open, ceilings are always permeable, and calls for help are always answered for people who are marginalized
    - Susan McPherson, business owner and leader in corporate social responsibility
- everyone believes that coping with hard realities and feelings does not disqualify you from a happy life
    - Vivian Nunez, writer and founder of Too Damn Young
- every girl knows that she is valuable and powerful to achieve her goals and dreams
    - Opal Vadhan, executive assistant to former secretary of state Hillary Rodham Clinton

Play around with different ideas until one makes your heart flutter. And if you're still unsure what your North Star is, relax. You've got an entire book left to think about it. Just pick a tentative North Star. Got it? Excellent. Grab a marker and write it down in bold letters.

Now that you have an end goal, there's nowhere to go but straight for it. So let's move on to fuel your efforts. We bet you're sitting atop a gold mine of resources without even knowing it. Most people are and they're too humble to realize it; let's dig in and see what it is that *you* have to offer.

chapter two

IDENTIFYING YOUR ACTUAL NET WORTH

IN 1973, LONG before Park Slope became an affluent New York City neighborhood of strollers and stay-at-home dads, Annie Ellman lived there in a two-bedroom apartment that cost her $240 a month. With a slight build and a fierce passion for justice, she attended Vietnam War protests and community rallies, joined the local food co-op, and campaigned for change. In her free time, you'd also find her taking martial arts classes, where she thrived.

At twenty-three, she already knew that she wanted to create change—to do *more* for her community—but she wasn't sure exactly how. The answer presented itself through her practice as a martial artist, at a studio where she was studying in Manhattan. Friends of friends—all women—started asking Annie if she would hold classes for them in Brooklyn. Martial arts provide endless benefits, from the practical aspects of self-defense and strength to the less obvious ones, like peace of mind and confidence. But at the time, the field was practically inaccessible to women. Annie knew that access to these classes was important, and she wanted to say *yes* to the women asking, but there was a voice in her brain telling her she wasn't the right one for the job. "I didn't feel experienced enough. I didn't want to do it by myself," she says. She went to her own instructor and asked for advice, sure that he, too, would see that she couldn't teach by herself. But he saw the potential Annie couldn't, and he encouraged her to get started. Next, she talked through the idea with her friend and teacher Nadia Telsey, who was teaching classes for women in Manhattan. Nadia assured Annie she already had everything she needed within herself to take on this challenge.

The first class Annie taught was in a church basement with twenty eager participants. She was so nervous she wrote out every single thing she would say out loud and clutched the papers as she taught the class. But even through her nervousness, she could feel an electricity in the air that energized her. Here was a space filled with women who were raising their voices, using their bodies, and finding their strength. Something was happening.

By the following year, Annie and Nadia had partnered up and started teaching classes for women in Brooklyn. They taught classes full-time, charged low fees by also collecting donations from the community, and rented different spaces before finally settling into their own dojo in the late seventies. Eventually, their community project turned into the Center for Anti-Violence Education (CAE), a social justice and self-defense nonprofit. We're so amazed by how they did all this *before* social media and when New York City was less friendly to entrepreneurial women, without the coworking spaces and meet-ups we're used to today. Without an online community to crowdsource their needs, they still had their word-of-mouth neighborhood network, which has always been a powerful resource. They started with small steps and stayed true to a shared goal to support community members struggling with violence.

To date, CAE has worked with and trained tens of thousands of women, people with disabilities, LGBTQ+ people, homeless youth, and more, teaching self-defense as a means of empowerment. The best part? CAE can stand on its own, no longer relying on Annie or Nadia to create its impact. After Nadia left the organization in the eighties, Annie found herself once again alone in teaching her classes, and she began training new teachers to work with her. This time, though, she wasn't nervous—she knew she could do it. *This* time, she was training teachers so that the organization could live on for generations (and so she could occasionally take a vacation). Today, the organization has trained more than two hundred people (many of them survivors of violence themselves) to teach self-defense. Annie, who left the organization in 2018, can continue her own community activism knowing that CAE thrives in her absence. What an incredible legacy.

THINK LIKE A FOUNDER

Like many people, we draw inspiration from founders of companies and organizations, particularly ones like Annie and Nadia, who learned to serve their vision and manage their relationship as cofounders with intention and focus. What founders teach us is how to see possibilities before plausibility. Have you ever gotten hooked on a "crazy" idea—to take off on an international trip or to run a marathon or to adopt a puppy—before fully thinking through how you'll actually pull it off? For sure, we all have. As you know from experience, that kind of impulsivity can be genius, or it can lead to heartache. We end up harnessing the impulsive spirit in a positive way when we let it make us curious. When we give ourselves the time to dwell in the possibilities before judging them, we open our minds and get far enough away from the pesky inner critic who always wants to shut us down and say, "There's no way you can do that!" A curious mind asks, "What would it take to do that?"

You don't have to launch an entire initiative or organization to think like an entrepreneur. Even if you aren't interested in founder or cofounder being your job title, challenge yourself to think like a social entrepreneur as you design your Impact Plan. We all get to be the chief executive and decision maker of our own legacy. To tease out your options, let's start building a Possibilities List, just for fun.

Look at your North Star, and imagine you don't have any limits. Think like a visionary—because anyone with an Impact Plan is one. What are the possible actions someone can take in pursuit of your ultimate end goal? Remember: Don't get caught up in the plausibility of the ideas. You're imagining what *any* person could do to push toward that North Star. You're unleashing your creativity, not judging whether the doer should be you. Imagine you're helping your best friend or role model come up with these ideas. By the time you're finished, you should have a list of ideas that encompasses the small, everyday actions, all the way up to some big, audacious ones. ✳2

In this way, the boldest ideas can come out to play with the simple ones. Here are a few possibilities we borrowed from someone whose North Star is a world where good healthcare and wellness are the norm, not luxuries:

- Start a podcast to educate people about healthier living
- Launch a social media campaign to drive awareness of breast cancer screenings
- Get trained as a cardio dance instructor and offer free classes in the community
- Start a community garden that produces vegetables for the neighborhood
- Start a birthday fundraiser for Yoga Foster, which brings yoga and mindfulness to classrooms
- Join the board of a healthcare tech start-up
- Become an ambassador for a global health organization and leverage social platforms to drive awareness and funds

If you're like us, a voice in your head waits to squash any idea that feels too ambitious to achieve with the immediate resources you have . . . before you even have a chance to make it viable. After all, you can break down any big goal into smaller pieces and an attainable first step.

So, when either of us doubts ourselves, we remove ourselves from the equation. Then we imagine all the possibilities a smart, capable person could theoretically take on, from the small (write a blog post) to the audacious (launch a global petition). For us, an example was, "The cofounders of a successful nonprofit could write a book to share their knowledge and inspire more change"—we believed that statement before we believed *we* could do it. You might not envision yourself running for a local office or organizing a smashing benefit concert, but there's nothing to stop an anonymous *someone* from pulling it off, now or in a couple of years' time. Seeing all of the possibilities laid out will help you to dream bigger and begin to picture yourself in the shoes of that changemaker you imagined.

Hold this Possibilities List close, and daydream about it when you can, because we'll come back to it soon.

RESOURCE ROUND-UP

Has a friend or colleague ever spoken about why you're so valued, and made you realize you had strengths and talents you didn't even recognize? It's so much easier for others to see what we offer, and as a result, we often underestimate ourselves. Eight out of ten times, when either of us is speaking with an interested volunteer, we find they dramatically undervalue their "net worth"—what it is they can offer others.

Resources are what you can "spend" or trade in to make an impact. There is really no limitation on what counts as a resource, so long as it fills a need. Money is obvious but not the most precious. You can always find more, whereas time is limited and you never get it back. Some resources you can buy, like a spacious apartment or access to a car, whereas others, such as a network or skills you've honed over a lifetime or the quirky hobby you have on the side, are priceless.

Another obstacle we see is when people have resources and don't spend them where their values align and North Star points (and yes, we've been guilty of this, too, such as when we shop where it's convenient rather than where it could boost a woman-owned business).

The legendary fundraising guru at the University of Notre Dame, James W. Frick, once said, "Don't tell me where your priorities are. Show me where you spend your money and I'll tell you what they are." His point doesn't just apply to money; he could have said the same about how you spend your time, who you hang around, what you post on social media. Those decisions are all tied to resources and reflect what you make a priority in your life. Your Impact Plan ultimately keeps you honest on what matters to you, much in the way Frick did with people in his community who would say one thing was important to them but then do another.

Given how revealing your resources can be, now would be a good time to bring them into the light. Let's go through some high-value resource areas and see how you cash in:

Experience. Here's a resource unique to you because no one else has it: your personal experience, the reasons for your North Star. When you have overcome adversity, learned how to cope with an illness or loss, survived a tragedy, or navigated a system that wasn't set up for your success, you have something to offer. After you've had the chance to process what you have been through, your story can be impactful to those who identify with your challenge or who should be an ally.

This resource certainly is not "free." It may have taken lots of therapy or medical treatment, or hundreds of hours journaling, mentorship, crying your eyes out, or talking through hardship with confidantes, just to arrive at the place in which sharing is therapeutic to you, helpful to others, and powerful on an advocacy agenda.

Celebrities with millions of followers and media platforms regularly move the needle as advocates, encouraging health checkups and creating conversation (and even changing the culture) around subjects that are taboo or uncomfortable. Think Gabrielle Union and infertility, Angelina Jolie and the *BRCA* gene, Justin Baldoni and men's vulnerability,

Michael J. Fox and Parkinson's disease . . . the list goes on. *Good Morning America* host Robin Roberts lives by her late mother's mantra to "make your mess your message." By sharing her experience fighting breast cancer and the rare blood disorder myelodysplastic syndrome (MDS) on network television, she has inspired more people to undergo breast cancer screening and donate bone marrow for transplant.

Opening up about adversity that is not obvious to the public can take even more courage. The day before Thanksgiving 2019, actress Melissa Benoist, best known for her role in *Glee* and playing the title hero in *Supergirl*, posted a video on her Instagram story titled "Life Isn't Always What It Seems." She read aloud a piece she had written about her experience with intimate partner violence, which affects one in four women in the US. It took her several years after the incident to talk about it in a way that she felt could serve others. She tagged Futures Without Violence in her post so that anyone who recognized their own reality in her examples would know where to find help.

Kiersten Stewart, who has served as the director of public policy and advocacy at Futures Without Violence for two decades, says that survivor stories have always been powerful in raising funds and awareness, appealing to legislators, and helping others heal. Melissa's post brought a spike of twenty-three hundred new Instagram followers to Futures Without Violence and sparked a media conversation that allowed the organization to talk about the issue and how people can get help. "Your story belongs to no one but you," Kiersten says, reminding anyone of what a personal choice it is to leverage their lived experience for advocacy. If you use your story, Kiersten's advice is this: "Share only what you are comfortable with the whole world knowing," even if you are only posting it in a private group. "If the answer is yes, you are comfortable, then if you want to share, share your truth," Kiersten says. "Don't try to run your own metrics on how to make it more impactful; don't change the language based on getting more likes or comments." One easy action you can do to increase your impact is to link your story to an organization or hotline that can help others going through a similar situation.

You don't need traditional fame in order for your experience to have a powerful effect on others. Hitha Palepu, CEO of pharmaceutical company Rho and an angel investor, started a blog that became well known for its travel tips and lifestyle guides. But after she experienced fertility difficulties, including a miscarriage and, eventually, postpartum depression, she realized that the platform she built could be useful. "It was lonely and scary," she says. "I didn't know that postpartum was even what I was feeling. And with my miscarriage . . . one in three women is going to experience a miscarriage, and we're expected to go on like nothing happened. I felt so lonely and I didn't want anybody else to feel that way."

Hitha published blog posts describing the unfiltered details of her experience so people would benefit from the knowledge if they ever had to go through similar procedures. She opens up honestly to her Instagram followers about her life experiences, and she now regularly speaks on these topics on panels and stages, reaching even more women in the process. She says she believes "the more we talk, the more empathetic we can all be. In a time when everything feels so divided, it's important to talk about the things we can empathize on."

Negative experiences can also launch legal precedents that make a difference for others. In 2009, Micah Fialka-Feldman learned that lesson after he arrived at university, only to find that the administration was denying him student housing on the premise that, because of his intellectual disability, he was not a "degree-seeking student."

By that point, Micah had been an activist for many years already, making sure that people with disabilities know their rights and how to advocate for themselves. He was on a local Kids as Self-Advocates (KASA) board at his high school, and he made one-pagers with tips for people with intellectual disabilities to talk to their doctors.

So when Oakland University in Michigan refused to allow him to live in the dorms, he sued. "I was capable of living in the dorms," Micah says. "They were trying to say I wasn't, but I was able to live on my own. I tried to go to the Board of Trustees. I tried to go to the vice president of the university, and they kept saying *no*. I had rallies; I had people write letters; I had many people that fought; and they [the university] kept saying *no, no, no.*"

It thrilled Micah when he won the case because it meant that no university would be able to discriminate against people with intellectual disabilities and bar them from university housing. Today, he co-teaches classes at Syracuse University in disability studies and specialized education, carrying his North Star with him into the work that he does every day.

Micah is one of many who has used the law for social change. After working as a manager at a Goodyear Tire & Rubber Company plant in Alabama for nineteen years, Lilly Ledbetter received an anonymous note that informed her she was making 40 percent less—thousands less per year—than the men in the same position as hers. She realized this only as she was two years from retirement. When she sued her employer, the federal court awarded her a $3.8 million settlement, but Goodyear appealed. Ultimately, the Supreme Court overturned the decision, because employees had to file discrimination cases within 180 days from the start of it happening, regardless of when they found out. Justice Ruth Bader Ginsburg, however, dissented, and a fight to change the statute of limitations ensued so this would never happen again. Thanks in part to Ledbetter's advocacy, in 2009 President Barack Obama's first official piece of legislation was signing the Lilly Ledbetter Fair Pay Act of 2009 into law, which resets the clock by saying that wage discrimination cases can be filed within 180 days of the last paycheck in which the discrimination occurs. Ledbetter remains a fierce champion for pay equity and is proof that one person's story can set a whole new precedent.

On your own Instagram or Facebook feed, there are undoubtedly examples of friends struggling with depression, infertility, or grief, friends who have chosen to have an abortion, who have an illness, or who breastfeed publicly, and they are posting about it. When done with intention (and not for the payoff of "likes" and self-validation), their vulnerability can chip away at stigma, helping to gradually shift attitudes, personalize political issues, and build community among others facing the same challenges.

Your experience is also valuable when it comes to mentorship and representation, in shaping what young people, especially, imagine to be possible in their own lives. Consider how you can leverage your experience, whether you make a formal commitment to mentor regularly, casually show up for a Career Day, or publish and distribute your story to a wider audience.

Network. It's all about who you know. Some of us are natural connectors, and that is a valuable resource. Whether you belong to an alumni network, you are a member of various clubs and groups, or you're just great at staying in touch, people power is one of the best ways to drive change. Do you often find yourself saying, "I know exactly who you should meet; let me email you both"? Is your calendar brimming with coffee meetings and breakfasts? Are you on the ball with thank-you notes? Do you get a ton of birthday messages every year? Signs point to you being a connector—and there's an easy way to use that power for good, by connecting people aligned with your North Star to create powerful alliances, coalitions, or relationships.

Imagine our pinch-me moment when we saw that Elizabeth Banks, the dynamite actress and director, posted a video to her Instagram page announcing that she was teaming up with hairstylist-to-the-stars Adir Abergel "to support one of my favorite charities, She's the First." She posted again, telling her three million followers that STF works with grassroots organizations around the world to share knowledge, power, and resources for girls. With a hashtag activation, Adir's hair care line, Virtue Labs, ended up donating $30,000 to STF.

Although we would love to tell you that we and Liz kick back with margaritas every now and again to chat activism, and that's how we introduced her to STF, this is only true in our dreams (at the moment of writing this, at least!). That might make you think we have lots of celebs in our contacts list, but it's important you know what is possible when big-name celebrities *aren't* in your circle of influence. So here's the true story:

Two super-connected women in Los Angeles, Arianne Phillips and Carineh Martin, worked their way up the fashion and entertainment industry, building an incredibly powerful network of luxury brands, filmmakers, magazines, designers, and more. Working for Christian Dior Couture and Prada, Carineh was constantly arranging for A-list celebrities to wear designer pieces on red carpets so that when reporters asked them "Who are you wearing?" they'd say Christian Dior or Prada, and all the celeb and fashion magazines would eat it up. Arianne, an Oscar-nominated costume designer and stylist, had an extensive list of fashion brands and celebrities to add to their client roster.

One day, it clicked for them: "The red carpet is watched by millions of people around the world, so that alone makes it very powerful," Carineh told us. "It is watched because it reflects our culture, so why not—in this modern era of endless personal sharing—shouldn't it also reflect our beliefs and values?"

Carineh and Arianne wondered, what if when celebs had the mic in their face, they could add, " . . . and I'm here tonight to raise awareness for such-and-such cause." The duo had heard about She's the First when looking up which girl organizations were part of Michelle Obama's Girls Opportunity Alliance. Our board chair, Tara Abrahams, was a consultant to the Obama Foundation and had introduced us to the team there. Based on our shared goal to empower girls through education, we have been able to collaborate with GOA and are one of four girls organizations spotlighted on their website. You see how networks and the introductions you make can set off an unimaginable ripple effect? (Because this is so important, we'll go deeper into how to grow your network in Chapter 8.) "With our company RAD: Redcarpet ADvocacy, we are every day using what we know and *who we know* to create social progress," Carineh says.

For this to work, you need to have the courage to broker introductions and invite people into your campaigns and causes. That feels like a scary "ask" sometimes, but good connectors know that they are offering a two-way street. People will say no if they are tapped out. Don't make their decision for them. Your job is to simply share why you care so much. You'd be surprised at how many people in your network are hungry to get involved; they're just waiting for someone to open the door.

Your contribution multiplies when you can mobilize the people you know to match your commitment or amplify the work. When you put out a call for support, plenty of people won't respond or will decline. That's okay, because just the right handful of people will jump on board with enthusiasm. It's all about finding fit.

Time. They say that time is money, don't they? And if you have it, there's always someone who can use it. From volunteering at events to answering a hotline or phone banking for a political candidate, there are near-endless ways to fill the hours. It's a good idea to think through what *kind* of time you have available. Is it consistent? Does it happen at the same times each week, no matter the season? Do you have a flexible work schedule, or is it dedicated time blocks that you can offer? Do you need supervision to stay accountable, or can you work independently, using tool kits you find online? You can spend time on everything from volunteering to serving on a board or showing up for one-off events.

For example, night owls could sign up to be digital messaging crisis counselors for the Trevor Project. These volunteers answer chat messages or texts online from young LGBTQ+ people struggling with issues like coming out, discrimination, depression, and suicide. The job requires a very clear time commitment of three hours per week, after completing a forty-hour online training at home. There truly are opportunities for every schedule and time zone, once you're up front with how much time you have and when.

Pro bono skills. If one approach is to offer your time and let an organization train you on what to do, another is to offer a specific skill you have and can teach them. Pro bono work is a distinct kind of volunteering, as it is time spent using a skill for which you'd ordinarily receive payment. Certain tasks that you could do in your sleep take others hours to figure out, if they even have the skills to do so. Think graphic design, video editing, writing a press release, generating Excel sheet formulas, building a website, reading over a legal contract, translating documents into another language, or performing at an event. These are all talents you took time to learn and master, and now that you have, offering them to a cause can save an organization hundreds, if not thousands, of dollars in professional services.

One of our favorite pro bono examples originated when Gap featured us in a campaign to benefit a program for women in management training. We had done lots of media interviews, but this was different. In this segment, Gap recorded our voices and played the audio over footage of us lounging around comfortably in Gap pajamas, smiling at each other and pretending to write our next big idea in a notebook. Sounds easy enough, but we still felt out of our element being models!

The director of the Gap commercial, Elle Ginter, is a petite, brunette thirty-something who commands a set, which typically has a male crew, in the most confident, thoughtful way. When the cameras weren't rolling, she talked to us about our mission and said, "Let's meet up in Brooklyn and stay in touch!" We took her up on that offer when the end of the year rolled around. We asked if she'd help us conceptualize and produce a video featuring four young women from India, Guatemala, Tanzania, and Kenya. Elle came through in a big way. She not only scripted, produced, and directed a goosebumps-raising film called *Extraordinary Woman* but also did it *pro bono*, saving our organization upward of $7,000 in production costs, *and* she treated STF with the same professionalism as she would any of her big clients, like Gap or Nike. In the end, she became our model for excellent pro bono work.

Assets. Think of assets as anything of monetary value that you have access to. Do you have a fairly large living room or spacious backyard? Great! You can host small fundraisers or gatherings. A car? You can drive patients to medical appointments or voters to the polls or help transport supplies back to the office after an event. If your workplace has open conference rooms, you can offer to host committee meetings. One of our coveted perks is from consultants who fly constantly for work. We've found a few who are more than happy to book us tickets with their miles so we can fly a speaker to NYC for our annual student conference or meet with donors across the country.

Hobbies and talents. Outside of the skills you use to make a living, you have the skills that bring you joy as hobbies. These can be valuable, too. For example, our friend Michael Gabriel, who lives in Atlanta, is *the* most passionate marathoner we've ever met: He's run twenty-six marathons and one ultra! Training for long-distance races is a special and impressive skill. In more than twenty of the races, he has either fundraised for She's the First (raising nearly $10,000) or worn STF T-shirts to raise awareness of our mission to thousands of people who cheer on the marathon sidelines. When the *New York Times* interviewed him about the custom-made costumes he wears in the Disney World races, he even negotiated a mention and link to She's the First in the article. There are unlimited ways to leverage un-conventional skills to fundraise and enrich changemaking.

Money. All you have to do is open your inbox to find countless emails from nonprofits and candidates running for office who need your money. For some, this is a tight resource, especially during tough economic times. For others who still have steady income and invest-ments, money is an option and could be more disposable than time. So let's consider.

The average amount a person in the United States donates annually is 3–5 percent of their net pay, but that can vary depending on income bracket and familial obligations. Nonprofits and grassroots movements *do* need money, whether for marching permits or community pro-grams. Globally, anyone who makes more than $34,000 USD annually is in the 1 percent of the world's richest people, given the extreme pov-erty in which so many are born. Half the world lives on less than $2.50 a day. This doesn't mean that you should feel guilty over what you have, but it puts into perspective why every bit helps.

There are ways to multiply your impact, like checking to see whether your employer will match donations to a 501(c)(3) charitable organiza-tion or setting up a monthly donation. You've likely heard that the best way to save money is to enroll in autopayments, directly from your pay-check to a savings account or from your checking account to a savings account. You can automate giving to a cause in the same way, without crushing your budget. Calculate 1 percent or 2 percent of your check and set yourself up for recurring gifts of the same amount. That helps the organization you've chosen to plan ahead, and it allows you to do-nate a cumulative amount. If you own a business or have a side hustle, you can create a "give-back model" that donates a percentage of your profits back into the community. As your salary or business grows, so too do your donations. We'll talk more about an effective giving portfolio in the next chapter, but for now, you get the point.

One contribution we often hear people mention is *passion*. Passion is great; we hope you have a lot of it! And it will come into play when you stumble on burnout and accountability. But remember when we said that a resource is something you can cash in or trade for impact? You can't do that with passion. It isn't worth much until you identify actions to put it behind. This can frustrate everyone involved: As nonprofit leaders, we've had so many enthusiastic people approach us to ask "How can I help?" Well, *we* don't know! We've never met you before. And unfortunately, we have very limited time to figure it out, without taking our attention away from the organization's main priorities. We tried—we would look at people's LinkedIn pages and guess what they might be able to do, but sometimes that isn't what they *wanted* to offer. If you've ever been on a first date full of polite pleasantries that clearly wasn't going anywhere, you can imagine what many of these conversations felt like.

So, instead of a bad first date, approach this as you would job hunting: You don't walk into a job interview asking them where you fit in. You write an impressive pitch and résumé, connecting the dots for your prospective employer. Somehow, with unpaid service, people act the exact opposite way. They think their offer to volunteer is like presenting a beautifully wrapped gift that no one can refuse. But your Impact Partners really need unwrapped gifts. When they can clearly see what you're bringing to the table, they can map you faster to their needs, and that's a win-win.

We've worked with people who offered their accounting expertise, event spaces, designer clothes, publicity skills—and for years, most of our photography, videography, and graphic design was done by two immensely talented women who either donated their time or gave us a significant discount. We don't always have a perfect match between what a person can offer and what She's the First needs, but it's easier to uncover the possibilities when someone presents their resources to us.

Okay, your turn. Think about each of these categories, and inventory *your* top resources. Don't worry yet about what you want to give at the moment or about quantifying any of them. Just think: In theory, what could you offer? What feels unique to you? ✳3

Once you've downloaded the full list to paper, take a moment to appreciate exactly how much you offer the world. More than you thought, right?

The easiest path to burnout is to identify all of your available resources—and then turn the engines to full blast on all fronts. So, once you've taken stock, how do you decide which resources to focus on? One of the best ways to do this is with a thought experiment in which you place your resources in direct competition with one another, because, really, they are! You only have so much energy; we aim to keep you running steadily.

To do this, we'll visit an imaginary playground to take what we call the Seesaw Test. Choose two of your resources. If you were to set them on opposite sides of a seesaw, which side would be heavier? Would they be perfectly balanced, or do you have more of one than the other?

For example, when one of our Impact Planners did this exercise, her resources were free weekend mornings, sewing skills, money, facilitation, fundraising experience, a church community, and yoga teaching skills. In this exercise, Stephanie tried to put the resources most in tension with one another across from each other on her mental seesaws. She placed money and free mornings across from one another, because though she has both to give, she knows that if she gives larger amounts of money, she may want those free weekend mornings to do a little extra work. Free mornings were the heavier resource. As for skills that take up that time, she can offer her sewing or yoga skills. Sewing can be time intensive, and she's already crouching her shoulders too much while typing away at a computer all week. When it came down to it, between sewing and yoga, she landed heavily on the yoga side, knowing that she could offer free restorative classes to women in her community. She used these quick doodles to narrow her top resources.

Having thought about your top resources, revisit your Possibilities List. See if any of those hypothetical ideas you had for an anonymous *someone* are calling your name. Do you see any in a new light? These ideas weren't for you to do, per se, but if they were in your mind, is it possible you subconsciously aspired to any of them? Now that you've inventoried your resources, it's likely that some of them appear more plausible than they did at first pass, or in the very least, you can break down any big idea into a first step that your resources match.

From here, another way you can generate possibilities is with the assistance of those who need what you can offer. To do so, craft what we like to call an Impact Pitch, a way of communicating your specific scope to others. Your Impact Pitch is a cheat sheet showing what you can offer an organization and movement so you can quickly match yourself to actual needs. You'll find a script for a sample Impact Pitch in the workbook. ✳4

Doing a self-assessment of your resources *before* approaching an Impact Partner is not only a courtesy—it's also efficient. Here's proof that an Impact Pitch pays off, from our friend and colleague Katie Riley. As director of strategic partnerships at She's the First, she's been on the receiving end of so many contextless "How can I help?" emails, so she was determined to be up front and specific in seeking her own impact initiatives.

Though she works for a girls' rights organization, gender equality is just part of her North Star: a world where marginalized groups have agency and power (and thus are no longer marginalized!). Katie has always had an interest in how governments can help or harm marginalized people and majored in political science at university. She takes a vacation day any time the polls are open to be an election worker so she can help voting be a smooth and pleasant experience in her borough.

Heading into 2020, a pivotal election year, Katie wanted to explore the intersection of grassroots organizing and voter turnout. Specifically, she wanted to involve herself in electing a Democratic leader but wasn't interested in quitting her job (lucky for us). She wrote a proposal to take time off for a part-time sabbatical. She framed it in terms of the benefits it would bring back to our workplace, because she'd learn best practices for movement building that could strengthen STF. It was the kind of win-win proposal you can't refuse.

To land her volunteer opportunity for the sabbatical, Katie reached out to campaigns and was clear about how much time she could offer and the skills she brings to the table: project management, event planning, data/systems management. Campaign staffers looked visibly impressed and pleasantly surprised by how open and direct she was; they're used to getting hundreds of enthusiastic, generic "I want to help!" offers that take effort to unpack.

In the interview stages, Katie was also clear about what she does *not* prefer to do—fundraise—because though she's quite good at it, it takes a lot of mental energy she's already spending on her day job. That ensured expectations aligned and she wouldn't underdeliver. As a result of her proactive and well-defined outreach, Katie landed a perfect-fit volunteer opportunity with a popular New York congresswoman's reelection campaign after less than a month of circulating her Impact Pitch around her networks.

Katie illustrates what our next step is—"plugging in" to movements where large-scale impact is possible. That happens once you've found your focus, dwelled in possibilities, and determined which ones you can resource. Think of it like putting together a jigsaw puzzle. You need to know what your goal is; your North Star is the picture on the puzzle box. You won't get anywhere without flipping all of your pieces right side up and organizing them first, and that's exactly why the exercises you've just done to make an Impact Pitch are important.

Now that you've got your pieces, let's put them to use and figure out how to snap them in with causes and communities that need them.

chapter three

PLUGGING IN AND PARTNERING

THERE'S A POPULAR fable about a young child walking down an un-named beach after a rough storm. Strewn all about her, as far as she can see, are starfish, stranded too far above the tideline and likely to dry up in the heat of the sun. The girl walks along the beach, bending over, picking up starfish one by one, throwing them back into the ocean waves, and repeating the process with every step. Eventually, she comes upon an older man.

"Why are you doing that?" the man asks. "Look at all these starfish. You're only one little girl! You couldn't possibly make a difference."

The girl bends down, lifts another starfish, plunks it back into the ocean, and looks him in the eye.

"It made a difference to *that* one," she says.

This fable resonates deeply with our human desire to make an impact, and the acknowledgment that no matter how small the impact, it matters to the person affected. And that's true, right? One-to-one connections fulfill us because we can *see* the change we create.

The only issue? That old dude *kind of* has a point.

That's why in this book we approach impact from two directions. First, there's the personal approach. We think about the small actions we can take to create change on the issues that matter most to us. That's part of finding fulfillment, of knowing that we're contributing more to the world than we're taking from it; we want our existence to have a net positive effect. You might forgo disposable coffee cups at the deli or mentor a student; you do this in your silo because you can see the effects over time, or because you have faith that it'll be combined with the efforts of others to move the needle. We'll come back to these small actions in the next chapter, and why it's so critical to do them. These are the starfish you're throwing back into the ocean, ensuring the world is a little better off for at least one, two, or twenty people out there, with an eye toward the cumulative effect you can create.

The second approach, one you need to weave into your Impact Plan for it to succeed, is to address the systemic barriers and challenges at the root of issues. This is a daunting task for those who don't work on social change full-time (and even for those who do), but there's a shortcut: Get involved with existing movements and communities to further your cause. Through collective action, you can accomplish so much more than you would on your own—not only because you have others with whom to compare ideas and share the workload but also because the issues most affecting our world today, whether inequality, climate change, political polarization . . . they all need more than a few well-intentioned people working on them to reach a solution. They ultimately need major shifts in attitudes and behaviors, along with changes in policy.

The good news? Researchers have found that it takes only 25 percent of a population—*one in four people*—to commit to making a change to reach a tipping point that creates a new social norm. It took a while to figure this out. At first, researchers only had observations of organizational culture and community activism to rely on, and they wondered what could have happened if the group was smaller or larger. "It's hard to rewind the tape of history and play it again," says Dr. Damon Centola of the University of Pennsylvania, who coauthored the study. "So what we wanted to do was study this experimentally and see if we could in fact look again and again and again, at how community activism might succeed or fail just by changing the size of the committed group."

Dr. Centola developed a method to create online communities and study how changing the critical mass size in those communities affected their capacity for social change. Members in a group were given a financial incentive to agree on a social norm, like the name of an object. Once that was established, the researchers incentivized a small, committed group of "activists" to push for change. After repeated trials, researchers saw that on average, the community shifted behavior when a quarter of the group pushed for a different name.

Apply this to the real world, and change that might have felt idealistic before suddenly sounds more feasible. So, how do you become part of the 25 percent? You sync up with existing entities, from community groups and nonprofits to social purpose companies, political campaigns, and other collective action platforms.

FINDING THE RIGHT IMPACT PARTNER

If you aren't already committed to a few organizations working from a local to a global level, finding an Impact Partner will likely be one of the Medium Effort goals that wind up on your Impact Plan in the next chapter. Here's what you need to get started.

First, we prefer seeking out word-of-mouth referrals and recommendations on social media before spending too much time getting lost in a Google search. Ask friends, family, and your followers for input on causes, organizations, or companies that play into your North Star. After you've asked them, bring it up in conversation as much as you can, with that person you're chatting up at a networking happy hour, your coworker, your local librarian, or even your favorite barista. Tell them you're interested in getting more involved with a particular cause—do they happen to know any organizations, companies, or people working on this issue? Do they know how you can learn more?

Your research has two goals: one, to identify which organizations aligned with your North Star are accessible to you using your network, and two, to learn how you can best plug in to the existing ecosystem. To do that, you *need* to learn more about the players already in the space.

After you've got your leads, and especially if you didn't get enough, it's time to google up a storm. As you browse websites, we recommend keeping these qualifying questions for your prospective Impact Partners in mind, and seeing whether the answers match up with the impact you're looking to create under your North Star:

- **What's their goal and what are their values?** Do they align with your own? How do they talk about what they do? Does their language resonate with you?
- **What does impact mean to them?** If they talk about improving lives, how do they know when they achieve this? Determine whether that aligns with their stated goals and with your North Star.
- **Whose voices are involved?** Take a look at their staff and leadership. Do they reflect the people the organization serves? Is there diverse representation?

These qualifying questions give you a reasonable filter for discerning the integrity of an existing effort. If you know the answers after scanning their website or speaking to a knowledgeable source, this is a strong indicator that you're choosing a solid Impact Partner. Your preliminary research might already turn up some options for what you can contribute. If not, or if you have a bigger idea, then you're ready with your Impact Pitch to start a conversation.

Your outreach for an Impact Partner could span nonprofits, community groups, political campaigns, or companies. To cover the bases, let's break down these different spheres where you could put your resources to work.

PLUGGING IN: NONPROFITS

More than 1.5 million nonprofits are registered in the United States and an estimated 10 million more exist worldwide. A commonly used synonym for *nonprofit* is *nongovernmental organization*, or *NGO*, which is actually a better descriptor. NGOs advance goals that are important to society, filling in the gaps that governments and companies cannot address. Truthfully, NGOs are not just filling in gaps but also responding to problems and inequities that the government and corporate sectors create. And they *should* be creating profit off of their earned revenue models or fundraisers— they just reinvest it into their programs.

There are valid critiques about nonprofits creating overreliance versus the benefits of governments changing policies to provide social services for their people, or holding companies accountable for environmental damage and unacceptable wages. At the same time, philanthropy drives progress and puts social issues on the agenda. This is why we tackle your North Star through your interaction with nonprofits, elected officials, and the companies you either work for or support with your dollars.

Let's start by vetting all those nonprofits people recommended to you. There's a myth out there about what a "good" nonprofit is: Supposedly it operates with low overhead, provides a low salary for staff, and keeps only small reserves in the bank at the end of the year because as much as possible was spent on programs. Don't fall for it! We couldn't disagree more strongly with all three of these criteria, and we'd encourage you not to seek out nonprofits based on them.

A low overhead ratio means that a nonprofit is putting substantially more funds into its programs than into expenses like salaries and office space; the missing piece in this logic is that without the employees, there's no one to develop programs, run them, or measure them. Low salaries for leaders and for nonprofit workers lead to exhaustion and brain-drain from the sector at large, forcing talented people to leave for a paycheck that can support their families. Running down your bank account at the end of each year and sacrificing your emergency fund, leaving no margin for error while innovating, is terrible financial advice—whether you're an individual, a business, or a nonprofit. Ul-timately, nonprofits need to run like businesses. They need to attract talent, they need to invest in all elements of a program (including staff) to ensure high-quality results, and they need to make sound fiscal deci-sions to start each year in a positive cash position.

Rather than review tax returns and financial statements with an un-trained eye, focus on which organizations impress you with *outcomes*. This is where you go back to those qualifying questions: What's their goal? What are their values? What does impact mean to them? Whose voices are involved?

Once you've narrowed your search to a few organizations you really like, you can start to overlap the Venn diagram of their needs and your skills and resources. If you think back to the image of *ikigai*, you're do-ing this to find the sweet spot between what you can give and what the world (in this case, a world-changing organization) needs.

Start with the needs of each organization. On their websites, can you find any information on volunteer opportunities? If you're look-ing at a global cause, these organizations often need advocacy or fundraising support that you can do remotely from anywhere. Local organizations generally have more options for showing up in person for time-based volunteering. Take a look at their staff page. Do they have a large team or a small one? If you're looking at a smaller organi-zation, with a staff of ten or fewer, it's more likely that your pro bono services will add capacity. See what their staff might be missing that aligns with your skill sets: Do they have a finance person? Do they have a data analyst? If not and one of those areas is your specialty, we bet they'd appreciate a well-defined offer, an Impact Pitch, to step in. You can also do a deeper review of the organization, noting whether their communications or campaigns feature strong copy, solid photographs, eye-catching graphic design—whatever your skill set may be, observe whether they might be in need of it. Whatever gaps you see, add them to your ongoing Possibilities List.

If money is one of your resources, maximize the impact of your do-nations by making them recurring and unrestricted, even if starting at

$5 a month. Many donors restrict their funds to the programs they like best and request the money not be used for salary, rent, research, or other "indirect" costs. This form of donation ties the hands of nonprofit leaders, who then have to fundraise specifically for funds to cover those salaries and office space, without which the programs couldn't run. It's a broken system that needs to change, and that can start with more donors giving unrestricted funding, no matter how small your donation may be.

BUILDING A GIVING PORTFOLIO

Whether you're investing $50 or $500 a year, you can be as thoughtful in curating a portfolio as a foundation with $5 million would be. You might purposefully invest in nonprofits, political campaigns, family and friends, or mission-driven companies. The goal is that most of the budget traces up to your North Star, while areas that don't are capped (which makes saying no much easier!).

1. Set a goal for how much you want to invest for the year, and break that down into your monthly budget.
2. Create a spreadsheet to track how much you invest and where. (You can also note any gifts that are tax-deductible here.)
3. Break your giving down into separate "funds." We offer the following categories for inspiration:
   • North Star Fund (a majority, i.e., 70 percent of your portfolio). This might include:
     – International—in lower-income countries
     – Local—in your own community
     – Aligned organizations in which you sit on a board/committee
     – Emergency relief

(continues)

- For-profit investments—in companies that support your vision for the world
- Political fund—supporting aligned candidates
- Personal Fund (20 percent of your portfolio)
  - This may be donations to your alma maters or places of worship, institutions that shape who you are today, or emergencies not related to your North Star but that move you to give
- Friendship Fund (10 percent of your portfolio)
  - Causes not related to your North Star, but they matter to your friends, and your friends matter to you! This is where you give for a friend's birthday or when they're fundraising for a cause.

Beyond volunteering and giving money, all organizations can use people willing to advocate on their behalf. This can start with simply talking to your friends and family about the issue and the organization, by dedicating your social media channels to them once per month, or by wearing their logo and using it as a conversation starter. Eventually, this can encompass more substantial actions like hosting a panel discussion or a documentary screening or organizing a rally.

If you glance down at your Possibilities List and notice that it's overflowing with ideas and you know you've got the time, that might be an early sign that you're fit to be a committee or board member. Generally, committee members are the worker bees; they work on specific projects as a group. If you have a strong set of specific skills and a good network, committee work (or starting a committee!) for a nonprofit might be a rewarding move for you. Generally, committees require a few hours of work per month, plus networking and advocating for the cause.

From there, you can prove your salt to move up to the big leagues: the board. In nonprofits, the board of directors runs governance; essentially, the board makes sure the nonprofit is adhering to laws and good policy, is fulfilling its mission, and is setting overarching strategic priorities. The board is also responsible for overseeing the financial health of an organization. And for the top executives of a nonprofit, like the two of us, the board is our boss. Board service is a huge honor in the best cases and a legal liability in the worst cases; board members can be sued, though this rarely happens, and organizations carry insurance to protect directors. The bottom line is: When you use your nonprofit board seat responsibly, the momentum you create is next-level.

If you're looking to join a board, you'll want to assess what you bring to the table. Do an audit of current board members. What could they be missing? Draw on the assets and perspectives you previously wrote down and think about how that would diversify their board. See if you have any connections to active board members, and ask for a phone call. Find out about the culture of the board and what's expected from members. Joining a board is a little like dating: You need to woo one another a bit, get to know each other's values and boundaries, before finally defining the relationship. In the process, you might find that you'd be better suited elsewhere within the organization—or, that you're a perfect fit.

Here's the catch: No matter how you decide to plug in to a nonprofit, outcomes will matter more than intentions. So, you must remember that if you can't deliver (whether that's by a deadline or on agreed-upon deliverables), you've just *cost* the nonprofit resources. For paid work, it's different; if you can't deliver, *you're fired*. You will feel those consequences directly when it comes time to pay your rent or buy groceries, and for that reason, most people don't flake on their day job! But for a volunteer role, it's natural for it to be the first commitment to go when life gets in the way. For any organization dealing with volunteers, it's incredibly frustrating to be left hanging, and worse, it takes more time away from staff to reassign the project.

The Seesaw Test and Impact Pitch exercises keep you honest by making you rank and quantify your resources. From there, it never fails to start with a small commitment to your Impact Partner to make sure the relationship is working for you both. See how much you can realistically handle, *over*deliver on it, and then sign on for more.

If you're ready to reach out to a nonprofit after having done your research, we recommend following the instructions on the website's contact form. Then send those Impact Pitches out!

PLUGGING IN: COMMUNITY ORGANIZING

We wrote and published this book during a time of massive political change in the United States, with abortion rights being cut down in state after state, mass incarcerations and family separations happening at our borders, investigations into hacked elections, and a Congress in perpetual gridlock. As we prepared to deliver this manuscript, we wrote from our own apartments amid social isolation and a global pandemic, along with a sharp drop in the economy. Philanthropy alone will not fix any of that.

As Gloria Steinem said, "Voting isn't the most we can do, but it is the least." After you've done the bare minimum, by learning about the candidates who best reflect your positions and align with your North Star, what's next?

Community organizing is a good place to start. In brief, community organizing means identifying an issue that needs to change, raising awareness about it, gathering people who want to affect it, and helping your group members be effective in the fight. Community organizing (whether it's to clean up an abandoned lot in your neighborhood, pressure food producers to treat animals humanely, reduce stigma around mental illness, or address any other issue) starts off small. Sometimes it looks like a few friends gathering for coffee once a month to brainstorm solutions or responses. Organizers distribute informational materials and talking points so everyone's message is consistent and the barrier to participate is low. The trickiest part of any social movement is that it requires many voices coming together as one; that's also what makes a movement so powerful. When that small group raises awareness, grows, and eventually coordinates with similar groups in their area and around the country or globe, large-scale change is possible.

Once again, these movements start *small*. When the COVID-19 pandemic began, you probably noticed spreadsheets, flyers, and Slack groups for mutual aid circulate around your neighborhood. The goal was to protect as many vulnerable people as possible by matching them with volunteers who would pick up their groceries, medications, and other necessities. At the same time, other organizers hosted virtual texting parties to increase response rates to the US Census, knowing that the data influences funding for healthcare, schools, and affordable housing and that communities of color are systemically undercounted. Often, community organizing simply looks like a safety net for those we live around or an effort to leave fewer voices behind.

Community organizing takes so many shapes. It can be overtly political, like advocating for specific bills or petitioning for change in governmental policy. You can become an organizer at your workplace by unionizing to ensure all employees have a fair and equitable work experience with collective bargaining power, or you can gather coworkers to put pressure on specific office policies you want to change. You can work on your block to support the needs of vulnerable neighbors, you can form a group to protest a new ordinance, you can join friends in picking up litter once per month. All of these actions are forms of organizing, and all create impact, step by step, at the community level.

At times, community organizing results in massive, ostensible change. In 2018, Alexandria Ocasio-Cortez ran against an incumbent for a seat in the House of Representatives, while still bartending to pay her bills (at a taqueria just down the street from our office). She ran a grassroots campaign through and through, knocking on doors, meeting voters at local events, and talking one-on-one with people about the issues they cared about most. She won that primary election in what was called one of the biggest upsets in modern political history, and when she arrived in Congress, she immediately set about her job in a fresh way. She opened the process by showing her daily life on Instagram and Twitter, and in doing so created a new standard of accountability for politicians. She also wants a rising generation to understand why their participation matters, so that young voters feel informed and motivated to call up their elected officials. More than that, the "AOC Effect" has paved the way for more progressive women to try their hand at running for office, at any level—the results of which will fully play out over time.

Another way to take collective action? Boycotts of restaurants, products, or services that discriminate against any group work when there's enough financial incentive. Money talks; when people vote with their dollars, they can create change. In a capitalist country, a drop in revenue affects political and cultural decisions. When there aren't enough people to create that financial motivation, or it's a complicated situation, you can find other ways to leverage your position as a consumer. After the owner of SoulCycle, Equinox, and Blink Fitness hosted a well-publicized fundraiser for Donald Trump, consumers balked that their gym membership dollars would inadvertently support someone they didn't agree with. But those gyms have countless employees—if consumers boycotted, wouldn't that just hurt the employees? Debates raged, and regardless of where you land, a boycott isn't your only weapon. As a member or consumer of a brand, you can also gather others who agree with you to write a letter to leadership or the board. You can use your words to pressure the brands and companies you interact with the most to live by the values of their main consumers. Meghan Markle famously did this at the age of eleven, when she saw a sexist commercial for dish soap. She wrote to the manufacturer, P&G, asking it to change its tagline that stated "Women all over America are fighting greasy pots and pans," because men had dishwashing duties, too! And sure enough, P&G changed "women" to "people" in future ads.

The flip side of boycotts are "buycotts": buying products to show support of a corporate culture or statements made by a company's executives. Research has shown that, although boycotts aren't going away, consumers are increasingly taking part in buycotts and being more intentional about the politics behind their favorite brands. When the sporting goods retailer Dick's responded to public pressure and boycotts by changing its long-held policy of selling assault-style firearms and high-capacity magazines, public response was swift. Influencers praised the store's decision and called on a buycott at Dick's. These upward ticks happen with sustainability, too: In 2014, a study showed S&P 500 companies with strong sustainability programs maintained an 18 percent higher return on investment (ROI) than those without sustainability strategies and 67 percent higher ROI than companies who refused to disclose emissions information. Companies that emphasize sustainability or fair-wage practices are attracting more consumers, which reinforces the business decision to pay workers well, avoid extra plastic packaging, and create thoughtful supply chains. We can use our consumer choices to be more values-aligned wherever possible, and thus put pressure on CEOs to catch up with what the world needs. It will take more than our individual buying choices to change our corporate and capitalist culture, of course. (This subject could fill an entire book of its own. We recommend reading the work of Anand Giridharadas to explore how government action must solve deep-seated inequities.) But thinking critically about how to use your dollars for better, if not for perfect, is a start.

In Guatemala, students at the MAIA school—the first school in Latin America run by and for Indigenous women—hold what they call "girlcotts." Instead of refusing to buy from a shop with questionable values, they celebrate shops they agree with by showing up in a group to create noise and chants, encouraging passersby to shop there. Picture it: A group of twenty girls, banging pots and pans, smiling, singing, and drawing attention to a woman-owned sweet shop. You know you'd buy a candy or two.

PLUGGING IN: AT WORK

We spend most of our waking hours at work, which is why many people look at their day job, and then at their North Star, and they question whether they're in the right place. Their current job may just be a stepping-stone to gain experience, or a good salary, so they can eventually transition into a more fulfilling role. Or they actually love their job and don't want to leave, but they feel a little guilty that they aren't contributing more to society. If you relate to any of this, we will help you brainstorm small ways to unlock more purpose where you're planted so your employer can be your Impact Partner, too. And if you want to take it even further, we'll suggest some starter actions to leap into a new job or career path that will let you bloom.

Getting your thoughts and feelings of disconnect at work on paper will help you move forward. Answer some of these writing prompts in your Impact Journal: What values do you perceive are held by the company you work for or the industry you are in? What impact do they make? Does this align with your goals? Does your employer have sustainable practices in place? Is it inclusive of diverse voices? What are the values you'd *want* to see in place? ✳5

As you're reflecting, consider whether there are small changes you could make, or a specialized focus you could take on, to find more fulfillment. Nikki Thomas, a real estate agent, became increasingly passionate about economic empowerment as she noted the wealth gap between homeowners and renters. As a result, she's carved a niche in a corner of the housing market that brings her more purpose: first-time buyers. Nikki believes home ownership is a way she can help people move up the socioeconomic ladder, and that's the impact she's making through her career. She is patient when educating clients about the process and even created "First-Time Buyer Bootcamp," a free educational series of emails with action items. Through her job, Nikki also has access to modern luxury apartment buildings with fancy lounges. She found that she can reserve those lounges to host wine-and-cheese nights to raise awareness for nonprofits she supports. All it took was setting up a meeting with her executive and pitching how this was a win-win, because it introduced new people to properties for sale, and it gave current residents a meaningful networking opportunity.

Another option, for those working in places open to feedback, is to foment change from the inside. Are there coworkers who would partner with you in your efforts? Can you create or suggest new policies to make for a more equitable workplace? Can you advocate for including social-good initiatives within the company?

At Marina Maher Communications, a group of employees banded together because they felt they were creating profits with no purpose. They enjoyed their work and were *good* at it, but they wanted something they could *feel* good about, too. They started an initiative called MMC4ACause. They launched a mentorship program within the company that challenged junior staffers to raise funds through creative events with the support of senior staff. The plan was genius, not only because they chose She's the First to benefit but also because it served the employees' interests, the company's interests, and girls' education. Employees stretched their event-hosting muscles and their salesmanship, which meant they were practicing their PR skills, all while getting face time with executives and sharing a sense of purpose. Over the next four years, the program morphed to be less of a competition and more of a company-wide initiative that won industry awards. They ended up raising more than $35,000 for girls' education in addition to funds for a girls' washroom at a Ugandan school that requested one—all because just a few employees got together to try something new.

In both examples, employees found success in creating impact at work when they: (1) created a value proposition for the business, and (2) got the buy-in, or sponsorship, of a senior executive. To integrate philanthropy into your workplace, those are the first two steps to take. This works best when your impact interests align with your company's purpose or customer base. An overtly political cause won't fly, as anything that creates division or controversy isn't going to be a win-win business case.

If you are looking to make workplace policies more just, you'll find strength in numbers by organizing in these ways. Join together with others and do your research to show how your workplace compares to others. This can happen informally or through unions, particularly when the issue is wage inequality or unfair policies.

And what do you do when your employer has values that directly conflict with yours? For instance, maybe you work for a company where the top executives are investors in conservative media and politics, and you're liberal. Even if you don't discuss politics at work, the company culture and decisions reflect a point of view in direct opposition to your own. Maybe you work for a boss who is self-serving and wouldn't give a second thought to your proposal to start an affinity group or a volunteer program at work. If your job is soul-sucking, then what?

First, let's just admit that sometimes your job is your quickest route to ensuring survival. If your job isn't values-aligned but provides you with the cash you need to live, no one is judging you for looking to other places in your life to create an impact. But if you're ready and able to look for something else? Here are some concrete actions you can take to make a leap:

1. **Create a list** of companies or workplaces that seem aligned with your values.
2. **Talk about these prospective employers** on the down low to everyone you trust. Even if you don't end up there, publicizing them as your targets will help your network think of similar opportunities that aren't on your radar . . . and might be just as, if not more, exciting.
3. **Search for mutual connections.** See if anyone you know on LinkedIn is connected to your targets. Make sure they are aware of your interest and ask for any pointers or intel.
4. **Position your brand around your North Star.** Update your presence on LinkedIn, social media, and your personal website to reflect your North Star. If your professional experience doesn't reflect where you want to go in the future, communicating your values and volunteer experience—what you do outside of the office, such as board roles—can help you jump from one sector to another.

Here's another takeaway from our own unconventional career paths: Focus on building career capital wherever you are. You can use your existing success to transfer your skills into another area. For example, just before Tammy quit her job in magazines to run She's the First full-time, she had received wide industry recognition as one of the first-ever social media editors at a magazine. While working in media, she also led a charitable campaign for the teen magazine brands involving donated prom dresses for girls in need. This gave her experience talking to several community-based nonprofits about their needs. Right before quitting, Tammy appeared on the cover of a trade publication honoring the "13 Under 30" in the industry. She used that accolade, as a twenty-three-year-old social media entrepreneur, as well as her side project with the prom dress–related nonprofits and her weekend volunteer roles, to establish her footing in new circles as a social entrepreneur. Similarly, what is a piece of career capital that you can transfer from your current job into your ideal one? What are the top skills people know you for, and how can you transfer them to a new company?

There is no one entry strategy for a career in impact. Jumping from for-profit to nonprofit organizations is common, but careers in government are high impact, too. Not to mention, there are nonprofit employees who want to switch it up and create impact from the for-profit side, whether in a corporate social responsibility role or perhaps at a B Corporation. (B Corporations are certified as meeting the highest standards of social and environmental performance, to balance profit and purpose.)

The important detail isn't the *kind* of company you work for—nonprofit, for-profit, government; it's the values your employer brings to the table. Should you have choices, let those values lead the way when landing your next gig.

AN ANTI-OPPRESSIVE APPROACH

We spent the prior pages talking about the practical pieces of plugging in. There's an art to finding the right spaces, but there's a bigger need to show up in those spaces in the *right ways*. Our world is full of systems of oppression, rules and suggestions that certain attributes make you a better or more valuable person. In trying to create impact, we need to confront these systems and see them for what they are: methods of dividing, subjugating, and holding people back from progress.

If you're reading this book, you likely have some level of privilege that you can use wisely to dismantle the systems that hold others back. For those who are white, straight, cisgender, able-bodied, and/or economically advantaged, there is extra responsibility to do so. Whatever your North Star is, systems and structures are to blame for creating the issue you're trying to combat, and so understanding those systems and your role in them is crucial in effecting real change.

If you want to plug in to a movement or create positive change in our multicultural world, you absolutely must:

- Recognize your privilege
- Practice allyship
- Share power

It all starts with addressing your privilege. This is true even if parts of your identity are historically marginalized or if those parts aren't obvious. To use Christen as an example: When you look at her, you likely see a cis white woman, straight, able-bodied, economically advantaged—and because that's how she *looks*, she's enjoyed all the advantages that come with those identities, minus those biases that affect women. Her reality differs from what you might see on first glance: She's queer, manages endometriosis (a chronic illness), and grew up alternating between a single-parent experience and living with an emotionally abusive stepfather. Like most people, her lived experience is much more layered and complex than the single narrative that may appear obvious when you look at her. These pieces of her identity make her most passionate about her work as a self-defense instructor and as an advocate for girls' rights. The way the world perceives her, however, has almost nothing to do with those unseen parts of her identity.

She often gets waved through by security guards checking bags at the exit of a store, even if the alarm has gone off; she's never been refused service, and no one has ever tried to imitate her accent. **All to say, privilege is less about how you experience the world and more about how the world experiences and reacts to you.** Christen benefits from the way the world sees her, and it's those pieces of privilege that she needs to contend with as she works to achieve her North Star.

Understanding our privilege allows us to stay curious and open to learn about the stories and experiences of others. We can acknowledge that what *we* have experienced isn't the entirety of possibility, and others have experiences just as salient and just as relevant to understanding the issue at hand. Understanding our privilege allows us to know when to listen, when to sit back, when to let others lead.

So, if you're coming from a place of privilege (you know, a white, straight, able-bodied, college-educated, cisgender woman or man, or a combination thereof) and reading this, where should you begin? Allyship is the next step.

To walk you through these issues, many other solid resources exist, written by people with far more experience than we have ourselves, so we listed them in the Notes at the back of the book. One of the voices we look to is that of author Layla F. Saad. She says, "Understand that allyship is not an identity, but a practice." Saad often imagined what the world would look like without white supremacy, and so one day, she asked her white followers to embark on a journey. She launched a twenty-eight-day Instagram challenge called #MeAndWhiteSupremacy in which her followers publicly journaled on their reflections around race and white supremacy. She turned this project into an online workbook, with eighty thousand downloads, which then became a book entitled *Me and White Supremacy*. (We cannot stress enough how important it is to read works by BIPOC [Black, Indigenous, and people of color] writers who can guide you to become a stronger ally.) In her book, she encourages readers: "I invite you not to run away from the pain but to allow it to break your heart open. . . . Doing the inner work and going into the truth blasts away all the lies and games, giving you a real opportunity to create change. There is no safety in this work. There is no clean, comfortable, or convenient way to dismantle a violent system of oppression. You must roll your sleeves up and get down into the ugly, fertile dirt."

Understanding your privilege and practicing allyship are ongoing work, but if you do them well enough, you'll arrive at step three: sharing power. Think about sharing power in the context of a relationship. In a healthy one, each partner cedes to the other in areas where the other is more talented or more passionate. There's an inherent understanding that it will all balance out in the end. In the world of impact, it's much the same. It shouldn't matter who gets all the credit, who gets labeled the leader, who gets quoted in the local paper. Which is not to say these issues will never come up but *is* to say that **the goal should always be bigger than the ego.** If you're looking for your state to update its laws on domestic violence, it will be more powerful if yours isn't the only voice at the podium. If you're working to ensure people with mental health problems have better access to health services, *make space for others to tell their stories.*

Whenever your work in creating impact feels lonely, reevaluate your approach. You need and deserve others around you for support, yes, but also to ensure you are understanding and advocating for the right change. Bring others into the fold whenever you can. The more, the better—and the more diverse, the stronger your impact actions will be.

This step of the process is to understand how you and your specific, interlocking identities can be of use not only in finding the right Impact Partner but also in attaining your North Star. As you seek to work with others, ask for feedback on your ideas or the ways you'd like to get involved, and check in along the way on how you can do better. You never truly "arrive" at being an ally or erase your biases or even become fully aware of your privilege; all of this happens in an ongoing cycle. If you keep addressing your privilege, practicing allyship, and sharing power, you can and will continue to do better. You *always* can.

chapter four

DRAFTING AN IMPACT PLAN

ASK ANY GO-GETTER how they keep track of their visions and progress, and they'll be delighted to share their hacks and rituals. For example, Tammy loves a good vision board; she collects magazines from neighbors and then cuts out words and images that remind her of big-picture goals for the upcoming year. On New Year's Eve, she pins the cutouts to a foam board so that when it's time for a refresh she can easily update. She then pops the board into a gold frame and props it up on her bedroom dresser so that every day she's looking at the cut-out words, photos, and mantras that remind her of her goals.

Another of Tammy's New Year's Day rituals is writing a letter to her future self, one year from now. She writes about her goals for the year in the past tense, as if they already happened: "This year, you ran the New York City Marathon, and you *crushed* it." It's a way of stashing what matters to her in the subconscious of her brain—or, at the very least, she feels accountable to herself, lest next year's letter opening be a disappointment. If Tammy makes a time-consuming commitment that isn't reflected in her goals for the year, she questions whether it's a priority and refocuses accordingly.

You don't have to be this orderly about your ambitions and intentions; Christen finds that stream-of-consciousness journaling, talking it out with friends, and updating an online to-do list can work just as well. The trick is *getting it out*. Putting words to that little feeling that pulls at you. That's the key to finally getting started on making changes—in your own life *and* in the world.

A professor at Dominican University of California wanted to prove this (or not), so she completed a study with 149 participants of diverse backgrounds. She split them into five groups. The researchers instructed the first group to think about their goals, and they asked groups 2 to 5 to write down their goals. Group 3 had to write action commitments for each goal, group 4 had to do the same and share these commitments with a friend, and group 5 had to do all of this plus send a weekly progress report to a friend. Any guess at which group had the best success rate?

Group 5, of course. Seventy-six percent of them accomplished their goals or were at least halfway there, whereas those in group 1 faltered. Fewer than half of those participants had made significant progress on their goals. This study is widely referenced in business magazines as validation for writing down one's goals, making specific commitments, and holding each other accountable (because sometimes, you've got to trick your brain into doing what you want).

Vision boards, journals, life trackers—however you do it, these are the secrets to many people's success and happiness. Yet even the best life-hacking plans don't clarify how to see the impact you're carving out in the world. That's why we've designed the Impact Plan framework you've been working toward in the last few chapters.

Your Impact Plan will fit on one page, the limited space forcing you to pick and choose what is truly important. Conveniently, it is also portable enough to tuck into your journal or tape to your wall, where you'll see it often enough to stay honest with yourself. Stephanie Jasmin, a career development manager at a public university and one of our most committed Impact Planners, adapted what we're about to do into an immersive experience right on the walls of her apartment.

One Sunday, Stephanie canceled all her plans and stayed put in her fourth-floor apartment to focus. After about an hour, she had covered the wall above her bed with squares of red, green, and purple. Looking at it, Stephanie saw all the thoughts that had, for months, been swirling around her head about what she wanted to accomplish in her life, in her career, and on the planet. What had felt so overwhelming was now tangible to her; it was no longer crouching behind fears, doubts, or other pressing to-dos. And all it took were packs of colorful Post-it notes to expose her innermost thoughts.

"Wow, I *am* intense," Stephanie recalled thinking to herself. Withholding all judgment on what appeared before her, she laughed in that moment, recognizing herself in a new light. "Everyone always told me I set high goals for myself—they were right!"

For a week prior to this exercise, Stephanie carried around her Impact Journal so she could do a mind dump for her Possibilities List; she recorded all the responsibilities, aspirations, and goals she could think of for her life, both short- and long-term, whenever they popped into her mind. In her bedroom, she transferred each of those items to a Post-it note. Green is her favorite color, so those notes signified her personal life—dating, friendships, family, faith. Red meant career— her job, her professional memberships, her training courses. Purple was for political actions—volunteering for her local councilwoman, attending a She Should Run training. She threw everything she was doing and wanted to do at the wall and then took a break. When she came back, she started rearranging the Post-its and grouping them by effort. Gradually, she forced herself to remove sticky notes from the wall to whittle down to her top priorities. She picked up every single note and questioned it before placing it back. She asked herself if it was in alignment with her North Star, if it had an outcome that was worth the sacrifice of time and energy. She forced herself to let go of the goals that she had outgrown or that simply reflected what others deemed desirable for a twenty-something woman instead of what *she* deeply wanted. She allowed herself to say no to the tasks that didn't align with her goals, freeing up more time for the ones that did. When Stephanie transferred these selective, prioritized commitments to a sheet of paper, in essence she had an Impact Plan, aligned with her North Star.

You can flip to the back of this book for an Impact Plan template (or find it at planyourimpact.com), or you can bring it to life with Post-it notes first, as Stephanie did. Right off the bat, you'll notice a few things about a finished Impact Plan:

- It's one page; just like a typical résumé, it should not be any longer—focus!
- It ladders up into your North Star.
- It's tiered by effort level: easy, medium, and high.
- It invites you to do some color coding so you can see how your actions integrate among the personal, political, and professional layers of your life.

First, add your North Star at the top. Remember, this is your fill-in-the-blank answer to "I want to live in a world where _____." So, to borrow Tammy's answer: "Girls and women have opportunities and resources to pursue their dreams." Your North Star is ultimately your through line, in all the chapters of your life.

The rest of your plan will be incredibly *specific*. Draw from ideas on your Possibilities List that have resources to back them up. You'll commit to actions that you can focus on for the next six months to a year. Each action is narrow in scope; for example, "mentor kids" is fairly vague, but "mentor through Big Brothers Big Sisters" is more concrete and clear. Then, add frequencies wherever reasonable; this would make your goal "mentor through Big Brothers Big Sisters once per month."

Let's start with your Easy Effort actions. We call these your Everyday Impact Points, or EIPs. Most people can rack up several daily, weekly, or monthly with little time and energy. Easy Effort actions become habits that make you an authentic follower of your North Star.

So, to support Tammy's North Star, some EIPs are putting monthly recurring donations on autopilot; buying gifts from woman-owned small businesses most of the time; amplifying other women's voices on social media, with an eye for sharing diverse voices; consuming media to stay informed of gender issues; voting in every eligible election. Don't underestimate these small EIPs! For proof from the history books, consider this:

Way back in 1938, an entertainer named Eddie Cantor suggested on the radio that people send dimes to President Franklin Delano Roosevelt at the White House to help fund a cure for polio (which the president had). A dime back then would have been equivalent to $1.82 in 2020; a donation that was still feasible during the Great Depression. "It takes only ten dimes to make a dollar and if a million people send only one dime, the total will be $100,000," Cantor said to spur people to reach into their pocketbooks. Within a few weeks, the White House received 2,680,000 dimes—$268,000 ($4.8 million today!). The non-profit known as the March of Dimes was born and used that money for research that led to the polio vaccine of the 1950s. After the vaccine's development, new cases in the United States dropped to fewer than one thousand by 1962, and no new cases have originated in the country since 1979. How's that for the power of ten cents?

Small actions will not create sweeping system change overnight, but they are a manifestation of your values, and easy wins are a sure way to build confidence and a sense of productivity that prepare you for heavier lifts. We get modern-day inspiration to stay devoted to EIPs from our environmentally conscious friends: Meatless Mondays and canvas shopping bags, anyone? Taking part in Meatless Mondays, for instance, is an easy effort that reduces greenhouse gases and has positive health effects. Other small efforts to give you a "win" and help you live out your values might include throwing a few extra jars of peanut butter into your shopping cart and donating them to a food pantry (for those whose North Star involves battling hunger) or dropping off art supplies to a community center in your neighborhood (for the arts advocates among us).

Though many of your EIPs should trace back to your North Star, this is one arena where it's manageable to add a few that help you feel good about your general footprint. Maybe you help an elderly neighbor with their groceries, or you're committed to only buying sustainable (or secondhand) clothing, even though your North Star focuses on something else. The beauty of EIPs is that they fold into your everyday life choices. Make sure you do have some that directly impact your North Star, and from there, you have our encouragement to add on.

With your Medium and High Effort actions, because they take more time or energy, you need to be selective of what you can do *well* and what will help you achieve your end goal. This is all relative to who you are and how you spend your days. One person's Easy Effort could be another's Medium, and vice versa.

For example, LeBron James has used his blackout days during playoff season—the days he stays off social media to keep his head in the game—to have his team highlight a different organization on his Instagram story. For him, it's easy to have his team reach out to worthy changemakers, ask them to submit video clips, and then hit upload.

Christen once used her Instagram for impact, and that was a Medium Effort project. Leading up to her thirtieth birthday, she wanted to raise $10,000 for She's the First, and rather than start a generic fundraiser, for thirty days, she posted a daily lesson from her travels, along with her appeal for donations. It took at least thirty minutes each day to cull photos and reflections that were meaningful. In the end, it was 100 percent worth it. Followers were happy to support She's the First, and they felt like they exchanged their money for a month of useful travel tips. For them, it was not so different from paying for a workshop or new book, because of the value Christen created.

Figure out what this kind of "medium" level of influence looks like for you. You know your bandwidth best, so be honest with yourself. As long as you have fewer actions in your Medium Effort bucket than you do under Easy Effort—we recommend no more than five—you're doing it right.

Now you're ready to focus on High Effort, and there is a reason this box is the smallest on the Impact Plan. We don't advise focusing on more than three goals at once—and even one at a time is okay. The point is you're giving it your all. These are likely longer-term projects that will have the most consequential impact on your North Star, be it on a global, national, local, or even hyperlocal level.

For us, bringing this book to life was in our High Effort box for a solid three years. Because we aligned our day job with our North Stars, that fits into our High Effort box as well. But again, to be a specific goal, that action is not "work for She's the First." Instead, it may be: oversee the completion of She's the First's strategic plan with the board, staff, and other stakeholders, and take responsibility for the fulfillment of two of the strategic goals over the next two years.

For both of us, it is important to serve our North Star outside of She's the First, too. This is particularly because She's the First is a global organization, and we believe it's important to connect with ways of effecting change in your own community while you're also thinking beyond your own borders. Earlier, we mentioned how Christen is a self-defense instructor in Brooklyn (through the Center for Anti-Violence Education, cofounded by Annie, whom you met in Chapter 2!).

A couple years ago, Tammy set a High Effort goal of finding a local board or council she could serve on that would enable her to influence and support policies affecting women. It just so happened that a few months after writing down that goal, the president of her alma mater, The College of New Jersey, called her. She asked if Tammy would consider serving on the board of trustees (!). At first, Tammy was taken aback, because she never imagined that would be plausible. In the past, her first thoughts at invitations like this would have been: "Am I even qualified? Am I too busy? Am I ready for this?" Self-doubt galore! This time, though, because it matched with something on her Possibilities List and Impact Plan, Tammy's reaction was different. Her first thought was, "This is a chance to follow my Impact Plan." Because she had done the same exercises that you have leading up to the creation of an Impact Plan, Tammy knew the skills she offered aligned with what the board of trustees needed. Her High Effort goal evolved from seeking out this opportunity to being a high-performing board member.

Now's the time to go back into your notes and look at the resources and promising possibilities you have; by now, you may also have solid opportunities that you've defined with an Impact Partner. Turn these into goals on your Impact Plan.

FIELDS OF PLAY

Todd Herman, a high-performance coach who works with athletes and business leaders to help them crush their goals, uses the term "field of play" to differentiate layers of your life. In this way, you can be intentional about how you act when you show up at home for your loved ones versus at work—or on an actual sports field or in your community as a neighbor and a voter. When creating an Impact Plan, the two of us love showing up on three particular fields of play:

1. **Personal:** This is what you do with your energy when you're not on the clock for your job. You could use this time for your volunteer work, for a side hustle, for your mental well-being, to raise your children to be changemakers, to spend your money in accordance with your values—for most of us, the list is limitless here.

2. **Political:** This is a field of play that is harder for some to navigate than others, given how many schools are lacking a strong civics education and the etiquette of "not talking politics" at the dinner table or around the water cooler. So, think of it this way, to borrow a slogan from 1960s feminism and Black feminism: *The personal is political.* Your personal experience—which you know best—connects to larger social and political structures. It's up to each of us to commit to actions that will make those structures more fair and equal, because all the philanthropy in the world won't matter if policies and laws perpetuate the problems. That's

why politics is its own field of play, separated out from your personal and professional time. Even if your work is political, this field of play encompasses the action you take as a citizen outside of your job duties.

3. **Professional:** This is where you show up to make a living. It includes your job, skill-building pro bono work, and the networking that you do to build your career and influence your industry.

To see this visually, grab three different colored highlighters or pens. Pick a different color to signify the personal, political, and professional and then highlight or star each goal with the corresponding color.

It's normal that most of your actions would be in your personal field of play because that's where, as the CEO of your life, you have the most control. Most people find fulfillment when their professional field of play offers them a means of contributing to their North Star, too, given this is where we spend most of our waking hours. As we noted in the last chapter, professional impact might involve leading one of your company's affinity groups, guiding its volunteer and pro bono initiatives, or changing a workplace policy to ensure paid family leave for dads, too, or comfortable nursing rooms for mothers.

Remember, you don't have to set your Impact Plan in stone; you get to mold it over time. It just needs to:

- Be written down
- Be left in a place where you can easily find it
- Rank specific objectives by effort level, to keep you honest about your bandwidth
- Show up on your three fields of play: personal, political, and professional

Head to the exercises in the workbook to fill out your Impact Plan. ✳6 To give you an example, we asked one of our Impact Planners if she'd be willing to share her Impact Plan, which you'll find in the workbook.

Another advantage of having an Impact Plan? It's an incredible gatekeeper. You know how celebrities and executives have an agent or chief of staff who vets all the opportunities that come their way because there are simply too many to handle? Your Impact Plan is like that. It eliminates the guilt of thinking you have to say yes to everything and everyone, because you can see the focused work you're doing. Overcommitting would make you risk falling short on your priorities. So, let your Impact Plan be the filtering tool for what you sign on to do and what you respectfully decline.

Recently, a neighbor tempted Tammy to take on yet another leadership role, as a representative for her block in county government. When considering it, Tammy looked back on her Impact Plan and saw that she was already doing so much; though being a block representative is a fantastic way to learn more about local politics, that didn't connect directly with her North Star. Instead, Tammy reached out to other women who might consider the position and offered to support them behind the scenes. This was a doable Easy Effort that directly linked up to her North Star.

Similarly, how about when your friends ask you to donate to their marathon or buy a ticket to a fundraiser or volunteer your weekend? Consult your Impact Plan and ask yourself, *Does this align with my North Star?* If so, this is a prime opportunity for you! If not, set a specific budget of time and money for what we call a Friendship Fund. When there isn't alignment to your North Star or preset commitments, bill it to your Friendship Fund. Eventually, the fund will deplete your allotted energy and resources, so you'll know when you need to decline. Trust us, it's a lot easier to say no when you have a thoughtful plan to turn to, because you're less likely to feel guilty and pass judgment on yourself (or care if anyone else does). You know the ground you're standing on.

Think of how this changes the way you ask people to get involved, too. Many people are uncomfortable asking for favors. But when you're clear on your purpose and invite others to join, this is not asking for a favor. It is presenting an opportunity. What you're ultimately doing is telling the world, "This is what I care about. If you care, too, and you don't have your outlet, then here's a place you can trade your resources in for the impact you also want to see." An Impact Plan helps you send up that flare so others who care about the same things can find you.

If you're like us and everyone else we've made Impact Plans with, in time, you'll find yourself underdelivering on some parts of your plan and overdelivering on others. That's proof that you're human. We'll show you later how to recalibrate.

For now, let's switch gears, shall we? We've spent a lot of time talking about you—for good reason, because change starts within you first. Now that we've finished Part I, you have a draft of your plan and it's time to dive into developing your perspective. How do you see the world? What are the biases you hold, either consciously or not? How might you challenge your assumptions to create the most powerful impact and better connect with others? Let's move on to examine your unique lens.

Part II

FRESH PERSPECTIVES

chapter five

ILLUMINATING OUR BIASES

Your own biases probably feel as if they're buried deep, deep inside of you: hard to reach, hard to look at, though you know that they're there. We all have them. *Bias* is a word often cloaked in shame, because these inclinations or prejudices can have life-altering, often hurtful, and even fatal effects on others. So people keep them hidden. We'd like to make the case that in order to create change head-on, dig deep inside yourself, wiggle your fingers around until you hit the bottom, and pull those biases up into the air to examine.

Biases make themselves known: someone crossing the street, subtly, as they notice a Black man walking toward them; someone asking, "Where are you *really* from?"; someone setting a building's temperature so it's comfortable for men in suits. It's much easier to note the biases of *other* people, of course.

Every day in our work, we see those small injustices play out against women and girls. Eliakunda Kaaya, or Ellie, as she's better known, is an unstoppable young woman from Tanzania. Ellie studied her heart out to become a high school graduate and got accepted into university, with scholarships to pay her way. In university, Ellie decided that she wanted to take on a leadership role, so in 2016, she set her sights on becoming the first female president of the student body. The only problem was the school policy noted that women could only run for *vice* president. But Ellie, being Ellie, didn't accept that answer. She began memorizing the schedules of various administrators so she could walk them to their cars, peppering them with questions about this "rule." She gathered signatures. She made appointment after appointment with the dean, waiting outside his door each day, and eventually, he said "fine." She could run for president.

While she campaigned, students and administrators kept telling her she was wasting her time and that she should just run for vice president—she'd be a shoo-in. But Ellie refused to back down, to validate the bias against women leaders. The day after election day, Ellie eagerly approached the results posted on the bulletin board on campus.

The male candidate had won.

Ellie could have caved in to the popular opinion that women weren't cut out to be leaders, but she focused on her success: Win or lose, she proved that a woman could run. "Afterward, many people on campus still called me Madam President, saying that I was an inspiration to them," Ellie told us. "To me that meant I didn't have to be president, I just had to show the university and community that as a woman, I was ready and prepared for the role."

The same year as the campus election, She's the First reached out to Ellie with the opportunity to visit New York City, to receive an award and to speak on the importance of educating girls to a room full of influential donors and connectors. She gathered her visa application papers showing what a strong community leader she was. On the day of her appointment, she brought her papers to the US embassy in Dar es Salaam, the former capital of Tanzania. She waited nervously in line, clutching her folder to her chest, rehearsing the lines she would tell the officer when it was her time to approach the window. US embassies around the lower-income world are notorious for rejecting qualified visa applications, functioning on the notion that young, unmarried people (and especially women) visiting the United States would want to overstay their visa and completely abandon whatever ties they had with their home country.

Ellie had official letters of support from She's the First and New York Senator Kirsten Gillibrand, plus proof of paid tuition bills that clearly showed she intended to return to earn that diploma. She began daydreaming about what it would be like to walk around New York, looking up at the tallest buildings she'd ever seen, when a voice interrupted: "Neeeexxt!" She was up.

Ellie stepped up to the window and the officer opened her folder. "You are too young to travel to the United States," he said. Pointing to the senator's letterhead, he added, "And that's *even if* I believed this fake letter was real, which I don't." He shook his head, handed her a letter of denial, and ushered her away from his window.

Crushed over her destroyed dream of visiting New York, Ellie walked out of the embassy and burst into tears. Today, she reflects on those experiences and realizes that for the world to change, people need to examine their own biases. "From the time we're born, society creates limits for us as to what we can and can't achieve," she says. For example, as a woman, you would make a lousy university leader. As a young African woman from a poor background, you *must* be looking to stay in the United States permanently. "If you want to create change, starting with the way you approach other people is a good place to start," she says.

Some biases are inherent to the human condition. In his book *Snakes, Sunrises, and Shakespeare*, evolutionary biologist Gordon H. Orians explains that some innate responses to our environment point to the evolutionary forces that have shaped humanity. Snakes give you the creeps? Well, your primitive forebears had reason to be wary of them. Also according to Dr. Orians, we inherently fear plants with pointed leaves or thorns . . . again, our cave-dwelling ancestors learned to avoid injury by steering clear of them. Biases based in fear have served an evolutionary purpose, but we can learn to overcome them.

Here's a case in point: For as long as Christen can remember, spiders scared the living hell out of her. She knows she learned this from her aunt, who was (and is) the type of person to jump up on the couch cushions to avoid a creepy-crawly. Christen remembers feeling a special connection to her aunt in sharing this phobia. This was all fine and good . . . except that Christen loved playing outside as a child, hiking and camping as an adult, and then traveling for her work—and she encountered some very, very large spiders.

Obviously, dangerous spiders do exist in the world and if you know you've got a poisonous brown recluse lurking under your bunk bed, living in harmony with it would *not* be our advice. But for those harmless, insect-eating spiders? They rid the house of bugs, like mosquitoes, that carry disease. They aren't exactly *welcome*, but they aren't *hated* in many places either.

Over the years, Christen tried to change her outlook. She even developed and repeated a mantra—"*Spiders beat malaria! Spiders beat malaria!*"—but it wasn't an overnight fix. For years and years, she would have to talk herself out of running out of the room with a loud yelp at the sight of a spider. Eventually, she learned to breathe and stay calm just long enough to find a shoe and squish it, letting out a yelp as she ended its pesky life. And, on a recent trip, when she woke up in the middle of the night and realized she was sharing her bathroom with a gray, flat, fast-moving spider, she took a deep breath . . . and decided to coexist. She's evolved!

The reason we're examining a silly bias like this is to show how you *can* change your behavior, even when it's based on an evolutionary impulse. Similarly, you can—and you must make the effort to—change your behavior when it comes to biases based in ignorance that impact other people. **Treating others differently because they don't share the same skin color, hair texture, body proportion, belief, or physical ability (etc.) as you—based on what you've read, heard, or been told—is an example of bias rooted in ignorance rather than in fear.** Actions based in such ignorance have serious consequences. Unless we consciously examine, challenge, and rewrite these messages, we can live our whole lives without ever questioning the biases that shape our worldview.

Our biases—and now we've established that everyone has them, so there's no use pretending otherwise—make up a large part of the lens through which we each view the world. They inform how we interpret certain information. Bias affects our relationships and how we interact with others. If we don't acknowledge and challenge our biases, we can make choices that negatively affect others. We may be more likely to hire someone who shares our skin tone, for instance, or less likely to buy a product from a salesperson with an accent we don't recognize or more likely to avoid a part of town because it "feels unsafe." We need to commit to learning and growing. It's a life-or-death matter. Biases toward humans can hurt, and even *kill*, as evidenced by the police brutality that catalyzed the Black Lives Matter movement and continues to threaten Black and brown communities across the United States. *It's imperative to challenge our biases.*

But how do we do that, given our quick, categorizing brains and how deeply and unquestioningly we hold our biases? A good starting place is to dissociate examining our biases from feelings of shame. In one of her books, author and shame researcher Brené Brown writes, "Shame corrodes the very part of us that believes we are capable of change." Often, when we recognize that we have a bias, particularly if it's related to race, gender, sexual orientation, or otherwise linked to how we judge others, we feel guilt and shame. We try to bury that bias deep within us so others won't see it. We want to think of ourselves as good people, and good people don't have biases, right?

Wrong. We'll say it again: Biases are entirely natural and inherent to being human. Also, biases aren't just *aversions* to things. We can have biases in *favor* of people, concepts, or experiences, too. For example, think of the times you got an internship or job interview from someone who knew your parents or came from your hometown or when you personally made time to mentor a student because of your similar background. We lift up people who remind us of younger versions of ourselves.

What we want you to do is recognize when you have a bias so you can yank it out into the light and study it. You can never truly *erase* your biases, but the more you work with them, the less potent and dangerous they become. It won't always be an easy or quick process, but addressing your biases starts with acknowledging that they exist. That is the first step to approaching the world and your impact on it with an open mindset. Good intentions only go so far; the people who make the most impact don't bury their biases—they kick shame aside, bravely address them, and then, get on to work.

HOW TO ADDRESS YOUR BIASES: DISCOVER, ACKNOWLEDGE, ACT

Discover: The first step is to recognize that you have biases in general, and then explore your particular ones. Begin by asking:

- Are there certain types of people who make me feel uncomfortable? Why am I feeling that way? Did I grow up knowing people of that race, religion, or background?
- Do all or most of my friends share similar traits, indicating that I might have a bias *toward* certain types of people?
- Does my family or friend group hold certain ideas without questioning their truth? Do I hold them, too? Are they rational and based in fact or could they reveal deeply rooted biases?
- Who do I most readily offer to help? Where do I give of my time and money? Are there any patterns in those choices?

If you want to take this a step further, you can become an actual research guinea pig right now. Harvard has developed a series of free online exercises that will allow you to test for unconscious biases in a number of areas. Head to implicit.harvard.edu, enter your email address, and then click on "Take a Test" to examine your biases toward particular groups or types of people. For example, when Christen did it, the test was able to pick up that she moderately associates women with literature and men with science. This is a common bias that people working to expose girls to the STEM (science, technology, engineering, math) field, for example, have to fight against.

Acknowledge: Now that you've discovered your biases, take this moment to reflect on the ways they have already impacted your actions and reactions. Identify the specific situations in which your biases have come into play. How might your actions have differed if you didn't hold that bias?

Act: Psychologists differ on whether we can ever truly unlearn our biases, but they do agree that we can change how we *act on them*. Consider reading new books, attending cultural festivals, or otherwise exposing yourself to fresh perspectives. Diversify your friend group, and start conversations with people you normally wouldn't. Be curious! If you know that you've misjudged or overlooked a certain group in the past, find ways to understand and appreciate their community and culture more fully.

Note: Dr. Jennifer Eberhardt, a bias researcher, MacArthur "Genius Grant" winner, and psychology professor at Stanford University, states that when we are thinking and moving fast, we are more vulnerable to acting on our biases. So, when you feel your own bias rearing its head, hit pause and take a minute to breathe, sip some water, or look out a window. Acknowledge, without shaming yourself, that you hold this bias and that you are choosing to challenge it in order to make a positive impact on the world.

THERE'S A POPULAR SAYING THAT GOES: "Your beliefs become your thoughts; your thoughts become your words; your words become your actions; your actions become your habits; your habits become your values; your values become your destiny." Slow down, and take a moment to read that again. If we shortened this weighty piece of wisdom (or word of warning), we could say that our beliefs become our destiny. You need to notice your biases because biased thoughts lead to biased behaviors, and whether they're unconscious or overt, they're equally felt. **Biased behaviors, left unchecked, lead to biased actions, and those actions directly result in exclusion, alienation, disenfranchisement, and discrimination.**

When you allow biases to flourish in yourself, you are accepting and encouraging oppressive systems—the opposite of what you designed your Impact Plan to do. Examining your beliefs and your motives is so critical in this process. We each must address our biases and understand the lens through which we view the world, because that's what determines how we act. Your motivations, too, can be rooted in bias: Are you looking to help a particular community because somewhere, deep inside, a part of you believes they cannot help themselves? If you allow that to be your driving force, you uphold the very system your Impact Plan is intended to take down. This work transforms an Impact Plan from an activity into a deep, sincere expression of your ethics and values.

Look at how far you've already come:

- You've documented the actions you could take in service of your North Star. (You did, *riiight?* The process doesn't work unless you do! Keep that rough draft of your Impact Plan handy so you can cross-reference it through this next leg of our journey together.)
- You've connected these actions with your deeply held beliefs. Your North Star is a clear reflection of what you believe should exist in the world, such as quality education, universal healthcare, financial independence, or political participation for all.
- Your Impact Plan commits you to specific, consistent goals that you'll pursue in the days, weeks, and months to come, across three major fields of play: personal, political, and professional.

It's time to stretch yourself further, and that leads us even deeper into the connective tissue between beliefs and actions: your perspective.

It's the philosophic core of this entire book. Your thinking will influence the way you approach your actions. It has the power to steer you toward the short-sighted path of good intentions or toward the tougher, truer, long-term path of real impact. Your perspective, or your lens, will direct the actions you take and your approach to solving problems.

People see the world in different ways, and that absolutely factors in to their attempts to create impact. We've got a couple of stories to illustrate this.

The first is a story of a very rich woman and a very expensive piece of silk. Several years ago, a friend of ours traveled on a learning trip to Zambia. The group consisted almost entirely of women, many white and of privilege, who had given to a children's program located there. On the first day, one woman seemed visibly uncomfortable as they visited with locals. The rest of the group chalked up her nerves to jet lag or first-day jitters. But the next day, she emerged from her hotel room with a pricey silk scarf tied into a sling around her arm. When others pressed her to say how she got injured, she vaguely said that her arm was hurting. The truth of it soon found its way out, though: That day, whenever anyone approached for a handshake or children ran up to her to say hello, she would stand back, gesturing at her "injured" arm, using it as an excuse to avoid touching others. She seemed disgusted and put off by the local people, and it showed. She stayed aloof and distant for the rest of the trip, kept her nose and mouth covered (with yet another silk scarf) when standing near people who were sick, and she refused to walk through health clinics that the group visited. Although her traveling companions had commended her choice to give money to needed programs, her presence on the trip cast a grim shadow over it. She didn't allow the experience to broaden her lens, she didn't develop meaningful cross-cultural relationships, and she cast a floodlight on how unattractive, stingy, and self-absorbed some Americans of privilege can be. She inhibited her impact with her attitude of superiority, lack of lived experience in Zambia, and unexamined racism. Her trip, although it was two weeks long, didn't provide her with a real connection to the people or deeper understanding of their lives. The other members of the group, embarrassed by her behavior, felt sorry for all that she failed to enjoy and experience on the trip. (Lest you harbor concern about this woman's arm, the group wryly noted that the injury miraculously disappeared at the end of each day when they all returned to their hotel for drinks and dinner.)

The challenge with biases is that they aren't always as obvious as a feigned injury wrapped in a silk scarf. In our early days, we once had a volunteer who visited a partner program and, immediately upon landing, she was so overwhelmed by "culture shock" that she wanted to return home. She called Christen in a panic after only a few hours. She had been nervous when her driver repeatedly stopped and asked for directions to the school. She was shocked to see, as her car zipped along the roads, people sleeping outside in the open air in the early morning hours and women carrying heavy loads of wood for morning stove fires. She had been anxious upon arriving to find that she had several insects as her roommates inside her humble dorm room. By the time she called Christen later that day, she was in tears. When Christen picked up, it was four a.m. New York time—the middle of the school day for the volunteer—and there she was, crying in front of students, lamenting that she couldn't handle living the way they did, even for one more day. She quickly returned to the United States, and you can guess what her impact as a volunteer was on the minds of the students who witnessed her outburst. (This feels like a good time to note that we no longer coordinate international travel for volunteers—more on that policy in Chapter 7.)

It can be incredibly tempting to look at the world and the people in it as manipulatable and changeable, especially when you view them from a distance or view them as "other," as the protagonists in our last two stories viewed the locals. A century ago, Austrian philosopher Martin Buber wrote a book, *Thou and I*, that often appears on college course syllabi; he explored the ways in which we engage with the world. The main way in which humans interact with everything around them is called "experience." In this mode of interaction, humans collect data, analyze it, classify it, and theorize about it. The "it" can be anything—an animal, a forest, another person, or a cause. The key is that the human sees that object as a collection of information, of qualities that can be analyzed and judged objectively, and manipulated accordingly. The woman visiting Zambia and the volunteer both approached their work and impact through this experience lens. The people they were "helping" were distant and their realities left unconsidered. This may have been unintentional or unconscious, but the result is the same: They viewed these cultures and people as "other," and they were wholly unprepared for when their worlds collided.

The second mode Buber identified is one he refers to as "encounter," the kind of interaction we should strive for as people making an impact in the world. In an encounter model, we engage with the *entirety* of a person or cause rather than "objectively" analyzing the sum of their qualities. When we encounter, we approach others as if they contain the same internal universe we know to exist for ourselves, in all their complexity. Encounter mode refers to approaching the world understanding that you are *part* of it and that everything else you come across is as well. It means that when you're consciously considering a person, a problem, a cause, an animal, or even a stapler sitting on your desk, you consider that your understanding of that person or thing is inherently limited.

Using this mode of interacting, of understanding that others are the protagonists of their own stories, means you can more readily find ways of connecting to others. That volunteer, crying in the middle of the school day, was showing the children very clearly how she viewed the experience of being there with them at school. The entire situation was occurring in relation to *her*—her feelings, her thoughts, and her needs completely absorbed her. It didn't occur to her to consider how it would feel to be a twelve-year-old excited to welcome a visitor from abroad, eager to show that visitor your school, only to watch her cry, with what looks like disappointment and disapproval, when she looks around or even right at you.

We began giving a "no crying" speech soon after that incident. Whenever board members or donors were visiting projects or programs, we'd sit them down and share this story. We'd say, "I want you to imagine that you've invited someone you've just met to your house for lunch. Your family prepares by getting the house clean, and you pick up a few ingredients to make lunch, which you spend a few hours preparing before their arrival. When your guest arrives, you welcome them, and give them some tea. Your family is nervous and excited to learn more about your guest and their culture and to share their own stories, too. The guest sits down, looks around, and her eyes water, because she just cannot imagine living in a place like this. How do *you* feel?"

We set this scene to help visitors ease into *encounter mode* and connect with others on a real level. It's okay to shed tears with someone who has shared a story or thoughts or feelings that have moved you— that's human connection. But crying *at* a person's circumstances as *you* interpret them? That's *experience mode* and is all about how you're perceiving someone else's life. That's what we want to avoid, always.

CRITICISM AND A GROWTH MINDSET

Being open to making changes in ourselves is a core component of what is popularly known as a growth mindset, the belief that people are constantly learning, can become smarter, and can achieve more over time. (It's the opposite of a fixed mindset, the belief that people are born with inherent, static abilities that time and experience do not change.) Holding fast to a growth mindset is *crucial* to crafting an ethical Impact Plan. It allows us to learn from our mistakes and change our behaviors.

It's important to have a growth mindset in today's world, especially within the universe of activism, when people can be quick to criticize and no one hands out ribbons for trying. "Call-out culture" (also known as "outrage culture") is pervasive, fueled by 24/7 news and social media feeds and so much division. We have limited space to get our points across effectively, yet we have a wide canvas with which to publish statements that go on public record, even if they're only intended for a small, closed group. When you're called out for some way you misspoke, misunderstood, or otherwise stepped into a tricky or problematic space, people are holding you accountable—often through public shaming.

An example of this happened in 2017, when author Chimamanda Ngozi Adichie answered a question in an interview about whether trans women were "real" women. Adichie had, until this point, been a hero of feminism and the progressive left, but her answer turned that quickly on its head. Adichie said: "It's about the way the world treats us, and I think if you've lived in the world as a man with the privileges that the world accords to men and then sort of change gender, it's difficult for me to accept that then we can equate your experience with the experience of a woman who has lived from the beginning as a woman and who has not been accorded those privileges that men are. . . . I don't think it's a good thing to talk about women's issues being exactly the same as the issues of trans women because I don't think that's true."

Her answer sparked a huge backlash, one in which trans people were hurt by her words, which seemed to be saying that Adichie didn't believe they were real women, after all. Others argued that Adichie was trying to say that trans women and cis women have different experiences, a point she tried to clarify after the fact.

She later told *The Guardian* she felt disappointed and let down. "I thought surely they know me and what I stand for." Adichie, and many others, question that quickness to outrage: Is it productive? If we're all working toward a better world for all, isn't there space for us to learn and grow along the way?

When you look at this case, you can see how quickly our outrage culture obliterates the nuance inherent in these conversations, and how it stifles the ability to have dialogue and to grow. If we collectively had encouraged Adichie to engage in conversation with trans activists, what could have happened? Would we have been able to learn more about what she *meant* to say and whether it made sense? Would we all have been able to use the opportunity to learn more about the experiences of trans women and about the language that can cause them harm?

But that's not what happened. Instead, Twitter and the media broke out into accusations and rage and made it difficult to pick up the thread of understanding how we should or could move forward together.

Outrage culture makes people clam up. You don't want to mess up and get called out; we get it. So, use your voice with two approaches in mind: First, remember not to engage in outrage culture yourself. When someone says something you disagree with, try to find the thread that will lead you to understanding one another better, rather than immediately launching into a tirade of who might be right. This is a concept from Black feminists who are rebranding "calling out" as "calling in." Not everyone has had the same opportunities or experiences you have, and if you see a way to encourage them to grow in their understanding, take it, rather than shutting them down. This applies especially if you're dealing with someone who has a history of showing empathy and social consciousness. If you're talking with someone who shares your values, it's counterproductive to shame and blame them for a mistake they likely wouldn't have made if they understood the full context. So help them out: Give them the context they need to understand why what they said was hurtful.

The only time engaging in call-out culture is useful is when you see someone showing bigoted or discriminatory behavior, especially if they're a person in power. Stopping those actions while they're ongoing is essential to creating a world where we can all feel safe; it's about setting and upholding the values and boundaries we need as a society.

Second, when you get called in—or even when you get called out—don't let it derail you. Understand that naysayers are the protagonists of their own stories, which may be several chapters behind or ahead of yours. These moments are opportunities to practice empathy, understanding, and deep listening. What are their reasons for reacting so negatively to what you believe is positive change? You can consider what they have to say, listen closely, and learn from their feedback (even if it isn't presented as gently as you would have liked). **Know that mistakes are part of the impact journey, and as long as you continue**

**growing in your work to leave the world better than you found it,
then you will succeed.**

To protect you and the work you care so much about from unintentional missteps—ones more significant than looking like an "ugly American," à la our silk scarf woman or the volunteer who wept in front of students—we will share more nuanced examples of how distorted viewpoints and a scarcity of lived experience in a particular place can backfire. Our goal, always, is to be transparent with you and offer as much detail on the lessons we've learned as will fit between the covers of this book. We'll take you back to Guatemala, where we found the inspiration to write this book. Except this time, we'll tell you a tale of ignorance . . . one that serves as a vivid reminder that trying to change a life beyond our own forces us to distinguish between good intentions and good outcomes.

chapter six

SEPARATING INTENT FROM IMPACT

MARTA, A MENTOR and educator working in Sololá, Guatemala, knows firsthand just how sideways things can go when the instant gratification of good intentions overrides careful consideration. Marta, who identifies as an empowered Indigenous woman, always knew she wanted to create a new path for herself. She worked hard to maintain a scholarship so she could be the first in her family to graduate from high school and lift her family out of poverty. In high school, she was part of a mentorship group run by Indigenous women who had also defied the odds to graduate high school and university and then to find meaningful employment. When Marta was in her last two years of high school, she started taking on leadership roles within MAIA, a local nonprofit organization ensuring her education. Occasionally, major donors to the organization would visit Guatemala to meet the girls they were impacting, see the programs in action, and enjoy the majestic beauty of

Marta's community, set on the shores of Lake Atitlán, famous for its stunning volcanic views and pink-orange sunsets.

MAIA, for which Marta now works, is effective in serving the most vulnerable girls in Guatemala because it prioritizes mentorship, local leadership, and building agency in its students. Monthly, mentors visit each girl's home and engage the family in games and activities designed to help them communicate, better understand each other, and work through any issues that might affect the children's success. Younger siblings, cousins, and parents all take part during mentor visits, sitting in a circle doing vocal empowerment exercises or drawing pictures that highlight their strengths. This ensures that the organization encourages the healthy family dynamics that are effective in getting girls to reach graduation. These visits also give younger siblings positive messages about the power of education.

When she was in eleventh grade, Marta was one of the students who stepped up to invite a group of visiting donors to her home. She was proud to be an ambassador and show just how far she could go in her life and to share her culture with visitors. She was aware of how transformative access to education, mentorship, and leadership training was in her own life, and she felt happy to share that knowledge with others.

When a middle-aged couple from the United States who had given thousands of dollars to the program came to visit, Marta hosted a mentorship activity in her home. She and her mentor were intentional about including the visitors in each empowerment exercise before teaching them how to make fresh corn tortillas served with eggs and refried beans for their shared lunch.

The visit went well, but the donors felt conflicted. As they looked around at the compound where Marta lived, they compared it with their own large, suburban home back in the States. They pictured their opulent house, the clean water that flowed from the faucets, the plentiful variety of gourmet food they enjoyed, and the excellent schools their children attended. Marta's family home did not have electricity, there was no way to heat it on cold days and nights, and the family struggled to sustain everyone's needs. The American couple knew they had to do *something,* so they came up with their own temporary solution on the spot to help Marta's family. To avoid putting anyone in the awkward position of accepting cash—which MAIA does not condone, as it gives students who live in locations more convenient for donor visits an unfair advantage—this couple sneaked a crisp $100 bill in a place where Marta could find it later, in her school backpack that sat against the wall inside the family's doorway, near where they had eaten lunch.

Marta didn't have occasion to use that bag—nor did anyone else in her family—for a few weeks. By that time, the family had moved on with their regular lives and schedules, and so when Marta's mom unzipped the backpack to fill it with products to sell at the market, she was shocked to find the $100 bill there. Because it was technically Marta's bag, Marta's mother assumed the bill belonged to her daughter—but that provoked a heartbreaking question: *How does a teen girl come across that much money in rural Guatemala?* Marta's parents were suddenly distrustful of their daughter, suspecting that she must have become involved in prostitution to end up with that bill.

When Marta returned home that day, she was greeted with tears and accusations. Her parents told her they couldn't have her staying with them any longer, exposing her younger siblings to such things. Marta, confused and upset, eventually left. MAIA found a place for her to stay and, after learning the story, came to realize what had happened. For weeks and even months, they tried to negotiate conversations with Marta's parents, but to no avail. Marta's parents are strongly conservative and were heartbroken over what they perceived were their daughter's actions. They refused to meet with representatives of MAIA or with Marta herself.

The donors' guilt and good intentions fueled that "act of charity," of giving the $100 bill. In that tiny moment—their eyes scanning Marta's humble home and their hearts aching for her—they were to change her family's life in a tragic way. But they never learned the destructive ramifications of their gift. This is usually the case: Most donors never find out when a well-meaning gift or gesture wreaks havoc on the life of its recipient, because of the inherent power dynamics.

Donors have the freedom to do a "good deed" and then to disappear back to their comfortable lives elsewhere in the world, leaving the recipient with unsolicited risks and complications. They don't realize that interrupting students' lives or playing a temporary role in a system that needs long-term development and stability is the very last place they should focus their efforts. The nature of these quick, drop-in visits eliminates even the possibility of understanding how their actions backfire. Nonprofits are also in a tricky position with donors who, in cases like this, want the feel-good experience of visiting a project, teaching a class, or swinging through town to meet students. If they don't have a candid and trusting relationship with their donors, nonprofit leaders—or any people in lesser power positions than financial contributors—often keep silent and hold back from issuing a critique of adverse donor behavior. Nonprofits rely on financial support, and their leaders know that funding can be a matter of life and death to their clients. None of us wants to alienate a donor who makes the work possible.

That means it is our responsibility as changemakers, building our Impact Plans, to question *ourselves*, in a rigorous and uncompromising way, when we're stepping into spaces we want to improve. It means listening to those who can lead us to understanding the steps to social change. Although many of us are comfortable doing due diligence on *others*—asking who is in charge of a project, how money is managed, what is the expected outcome, and so on—how many truly interrogate *ourselves* that thoroughly? That's why the challenging and sometimes awkward work we had you do in the last chapter, investigating, acknowledging, and working to alter your biases, is so critical.

After several months of persistent attempts to check in, the local mentors who work for MAIA finally reconnected Marta with her family. If the visiting couple had been open to their expertise from the start, how might Marta's story be different? What if the well-meaning couple acknowledged their biases and "encountered" Marta and her family, instead of simply "experiencing" them? What if they had approached the opportunity as a learning experience, rather than as an opportunity to save someone?

Like that couple slipping the money into Marta's backpack, one of the biggest impulses we must learn to wrestle with is our own notion of what will solve other people's problems. As we explored in depth in Chapter 5, we all have unique life experiences, filters, and biases that inform how we see, diagnose, and address challenges. We've said it before and we'll say it again: *Outcomes are everything.* That's why it's important to remember the solutions that worked in our own lives or communities are not one-size-fits-all. Not every idea that *sounds* good has positive outcomes in a particular context. Similarly, it's dangerous to assume that something we'd never want for ourselves—such as receiving medical care from an untrained volunteer or being taught by someone with no credentials—should work in an impoverished community just because they don't have other options.

As you dive into your own area of impact—whether it's LGBTQ+ rights, the environment, civil liberties, social justice, or something else—you'll bask in upbeat stories of meaningful change. But, we're warning you now, you'll also hear plenty of screwed-up ones. When you encounter the latter, it might tempt you to think, "At least I've never done anything *that* awful" (assuming you never broke up a family after being welcomed into their home). Although it's easy to condemn other people and wonder how it wasn't glaringly obvious for them to see their missteps, we hope you'll resist the temptation to judge. We invite you to go deeper and see that, on closer consideration, the reason they could not see what a mess they were making is because without examining their biases, seeing the difference between intent and impact is tough. *Really tough.*

This chapter offers stories of misguided interventions, as well as smart ones, and the lessons we can take away from them. Any cautionary tales are an invitation to learn so the rest of us don't fall into the same traps. Sometimes, you can even learn how to pivot mistakes or short-term fixes into preventative solutions and lasting change.

POSITIVE

Band-Aids: Acts of charity, consumption, or kindness that mitigate suffering; ranges from neutrally to positively affecting others	**Systems Solutions:** Contributions to collective action that get to the root of the problem by changing policies and norms
Misguided Moves: Actions that make a single situation worse for others; ranges from a nuisance to deadly consequences	**Systems Failures:** Contributions to policies and norms that institutionalize inequity and damage

SHORT-TERM ———————————————— LONG-TERM

NEGATIVE

Picture it this way: All our actions fall somewhere on a plane divided into four quadrants. The vertical axis represents a spectrum of positive to negative effects and the horizontal axis represents a span of time. Let's start with the impact of Band-Aids, as shown in the top left quadrant of this matrix.

BAND-AIDS

Band-Aid fixes include acts of charity, consumption, or kindness that mitigate suffering. True Band-Aids can impact others in a *neutral to positive* range. (The problematic part is when outcomes are actually negative and the doer doesn't realize it—like Marta's visitors who thought their cash gift would mitigate, for a short while, anyway, her family's poverty. That was a Misguided Move, per our matrix, and we'll get into that next.)

Giving a Band-Aid usually feels great. Our brains are wired for instant gratification, and helping others, with a random good deed or donation, can light up the brain's reward center much in the same way we get a rush of dopamine after drinking caffeine. Researchers who study brain imaging to see when specific regions of the brain are active have found that giving stimulates our mesolimbic pathway, or the brain's reward center. Couple that with studies showing how our brains light up when we're thinking about the present versus the future, and you see how people crave the instant gratification of seeing the good they've created right then, right there.

These endorphin-happy solutions are accessible to people. Band-Aid efforts can be quick and time-efficient, which is why the Easy and Medium Effort portions of your Impact Plan are probably filled with them.

Band-Aids, of course, have their cynics, who see them as lazy, insufficient answers to complicated questions. The critics of Band-Aid solutions will tell you these efforts aren't worth your time, because they won't actually solve the problem. Band-Aids, as in our example of disaster relief, are short-term solutions to help others endure or survive tough situations. Is giving a new pair of shoes to someone who has none a Band-Aid? Well, will it end the fact that they're living below the poverty line? Nope; it's a Band-Aid. Does a soup kitchen solve housing instability or poverty? No; it's a Band-Aid. Will providing girls in sub-Saharan Africa with pads end their struggles with accessing sanitary supplies? Yes . . . for as long as you're able to provide them. (Then what?) To identify a Band-Aid, just ask yourself one question: Will this fix the *root cause* (or the "evil at the bottom") of the issue?

Working long term to change a system of injustice or to address any other complex problem takes time. There's no feel-good instant gratification, no dopamine high about it. So, should you turn your back on Band-Aids?

Our take is to find the middle ground. Labeling a Band-Aid as such allows you to identify the root cause that needs addressing, and that's critical (we'll get to how to do this soon). We want to give true Band-Aids a little more respect, because they offer each of us the ability to make the people around us (and our planet) suffer less, each and every day. The purpose of Band-Aids isn't to fix the whole problem—it's just to ease hardship until more holistic solutions can be found. After an earthquake, wildfire, pandemic, or hurricane, all we have are Band-Aids like emergency funds, shelter, clothing, and food for displaced or unemployed people. These contributions won't address the underlying issues of the climate crisis, weak infrastructure, or economic inequality, but they are indisputably what people (and other living creatures) need at the moment. That's dependable relief. Rather than downplay Band-Aid efforts, simply recognize that you understand the limit of their impact.

Veronika Scott is someone who has not only benefited from effective Band-Aids but also created one. It all began when she was a twenty-one-year-old undergrad at Detroit's College for Creative Studies. She received a class assignment: Make something that people in the community really need. Veronika's parents faced homelessness on and off while she was a kid. She remembers absorbing their stress and wondering some nights where she'd be sleeping. "When I was growing up, it was about survival," Veronika told us. "I didn't even think about contributing back to my community." This class project was an opportunity to finally connect her lived experience in poverty with the problems affecting people without a social safety net.

Because housing instability had been her reality growing up, Veronika's North Star pointed her in the direction of people facing homelessness. When she told her fellow students she'd be heading out after class to the local shelter to tackle her project, no one joined her. To them, it felt a little dangerous and uncomfortable, even though living in Detroit, the homelessness epidemic was impossible to ignore. At the time, there were at least twenty thousand people facing homelessness on the streets of that city alone, and most winter nights in Detroit have freezing temperatures. After her visit, a proverbial light bulb went off in Veronika's head: People needed coats! Veronika taught herself to sew and designed a waterproof, insulated coat that doubles as a sleeping bag so that those who are living outdoors can be warmer all day and all night long. In warmer temperatures, the coat rolls up to be easily transported as an over-the-shoulder bag. Fast-forward to 2019: Forty-three thousand of these coats have been distributed.

Those of us who aren't inventors like Veronika have been a part of similar efforts whenever we've donated clothes or other items to a resale shop or collection drive. In the United States, for example, at least two hundred thousand teens have donated more than five million pairs of jeans to youths in shelters via DoSomething.org over the past decade. Jeans are a valuable item for homeless teens: They're durable and versatile. Donating jeans to teenagers facing homelessness won't provide them housing stability, but it can help keep their dignity intact as they navigate through school and adolescence. Similarly, donating professional attire to Dress for Success may help a lower-income woman fit into the dress code of a higher-paying job, though it won't magically resolve the burdens she manages at home. However, when the donation is coupled with the other client services Dress for Success provides, like leadership programs, clothing can give her a confidence boost that gets her through another day so that, paycheck by paycheck, she can work toward achieving financial freedom. Band-Aids, yes, but worthwhile ones.

Not all donations are physical items. Lately, stories about donating funds and paid leave to colleagues-in-need have gone viral. One woman in Missouri couldn't get maternity leave because she had worked less than one year for her employer (and because the United States is the only industrialized nation without paid maternity leave). When her baby arrived two months early, her boss donated eighty hours of her own paid time off to the new mother. Thanks to her colleagues' generosity, this woman received eight weeks of paid maternity leave. She's not the only case; coworkers donating their leave has happened often enough that it's now a trend.

One of our own fierce friends has a genetic condition that decimates her bones and has put her through several surgeries over the years. While in recovery (and still loopy on medication), she popped open her laptop and put her professional fundraising skills to use for herself. She went out of her comfort zone to start a GoFundMe campaign to help cover the cost of her medical bills, and her friends responded generously. This isn't uncommon. On GoFundMe, individuals have donated more than $650 million to help people they know (or even complete strangers!) pay off medical bills. Do these donations fix the underlying cause of astronomical medical bills or the lack of quality healthcare for all? Nope: They ease the burden in the absence of needed systems change.

So, you see why we insist on taking a middle ground on Band-Aids such as crowdfunding campaigns, donations of clothing and food, and reducing our carbon footprints. Together, we can acknowledge that these actions make life more bearable for many people in need, even if they don't address the underlying issues. We can stay heartened by seeing people engage in beautiful acts of generosity, without allowing ourselves to get lost in inspiring viral videos or hits of dopamine. We can keep our eyes on the bigger picture. More and more, you'll find yourself stopping short and thinking: "Wait. Shouldn't the government be taking care of this? When people can't afford housing or medical attention or education, doesn't that mean our systems have entirely broken down?"

Absolutely, yes! And we'll dig even deeper into those issues in the next chapter—but, for now, we focus on Band-Aids. By this point, we hope we've convinced you of their usefulness for short-term impact and their failings in lasting, systemic change. We have one last exercise to think through together, because as we all seek to make an impact, we want to keep in mind that *it's not about us.* We need to examine our own ideas of what will solve other people's problems and be sure that the recipients of Band-Aids have a say in dictating what they are. We need to keep *their* lived experience at the forefront of our response and be deliberate about why we are offering our help. This can get dicey, again based on our own lived experiences, biases, and intentions.

Imagine walking into your local coffee shop in the morning and seeing a person experiencing homelessness outside. He calls out to you, saying he's hungry and asking for a few dollars so he can buy breakfast. *Do you give him cash? Run in and buy him a banana? Do you hurry past with a quick hello? Do you simply ignore him?* There are so many reasons we may choose to give, or not give, in that moment:

You give because you want to ease his pain. You knew two dollars wasn't going to solve the person's challenges, but you figure it can at least help him through the morning. And anyway, can you imagine how difficult a person's life must be for begging to be their best option for survival? It seems like an easy choice to give up a couple dollars if you're fortunate enough to be able to spare them. This is the positive side of Band-Aid approaches; they do ease pain in the moment, even if they can't claim to fix an issue overall. Your intentions are good, you've acknowledged that person's humanity and let the recipient dictate what they need, and the outcome seems positive.

You buy him fruit instead of giving him a dollar so he won't "misuse" the money. It's a fairly common trope that you should never give cash to someone experiencing homelessness because they'll "just spend it on drugs," right? The issue with that logic is that it assumes the giver understands more about the other person's difficulties, when really, we have no way to begin to understand the priorities and needs of the individual in front of us. Does this person have specific dietary needs? Does the person have a physical or mental illness and, lacking support or resources, self-medicate with drugs or alcohol? Does the person deserve your judgment (or even want that ninety-nine-cent banana?) as you leave with your five-dollar latte and a breakfast burrito? This is one of the dangers of Band-Aids: We can easily fall into self-righteous, prescriptive ways of giving that strip away the agency and particular experience of the person actually facing the issue. (If you happen to have a snack on you, you can ask if they want it! The point is not about canceling snacks; it's about acknowledging the bias in your assumptions.)

You give money quickly to ease your guilt. One of the biggest critiques of Band-Aid solutions is that they exist primarily to make the giver feel better. (We mentioned earlier how the brain lights up when we do a good deed.) Guilt may seem like a "bad" reason to give, but feeling guilty about our relative luck in life *is* often a force behind doing good. What we need to remember when it comes to guilt is that it's okay to feel as though you should pay your good fortune forward to those who have less of it; but giving quickly and hastily in order to feel better about that guilt is unlikely to tackle the issue in a sustainable way.

You walk past the person without giving anything at all. Most likely, this resulted from feeling entirely unsure of what you "should" be doing. Maybe it's because you give to a formal program supporting people experiencing homelessness, or you simply felt conflicted because your North Star has a different focus. You didn't want to do the wrong thing, and you're trying not to spread yourself too thin, so you acknowledge the person with eye contact or an apology, but keep walking.

You probably wanted us—expected us—to tell you what you *should* do. Sorry. That's your personal decision, based on many factors, so we can't do that. But what we *can* do is offer you some tips to use Band-Aids effectively:

1. **If you decide to take action, remember to ask what is needed.** You can (and should) directly ask the person in need what would be most helpful.
2. **Examine the root cause of why a Band-Aid is needed.** This keeps your action in perspective, and it will help you determine how you can go about tackling the bigger issue with an Impact Partner.
3. **Band-Aids don't have to be fast;** use the opportunity to get to know new people working in or impacted by the issue area so you can better diagnose what's needed down the line. Begin to build a community for support and guidance.

Take this opportunity to review your Impact Plan actions. Mark those that look like Band-Aids to you, because they give direct relief but don't address the root cause of an issue. A way to check your work is to ask: Will this prevent the issue from happening again?

If you're finding a bunch of Band-Aids on your Impact Plan, don't sweat it. The important step is to recognize that they *are* Band-Aids. Meanwhile, you can continue learning how to contribute to long-term, systemic solutions and later add those ideas to your Impact Plan.

To detect the root causes beneath your Band-Aids, use these questions to guide you:

- Why is this Band-Aid needed in the first place?
- Is there a specific group in need of this Band-Aid? Why might that be?
- Many issues trace back to inequality, instability (i.e., conflict), or climate crisis. Is that the case with your Band-Aid?
- What could replace this Band-Aid solution in the long term?

By the end of Part II, your goal is to match up Band-Aids with Systems Solutions so that you have a two-pronged approach to your changemaking. Systems Solutions, as you'll see, aren't always obvious. They require research and experimentation to get right. Until then, Band-Aids give you the chance to work more closely with affected populations, and the organizations serving them, to ease pain and learn about the deeper issues.

chapter seven

PURSUING SYSTEMS SOLUTIONS

WHEN SHE WAS a teenager, Pippa Biddle went on a weeklong trip to Tanzania with her private school, primarily white, classmates from the United States. The trip organizers promised Pippa and her group that they would return home having built a library for a community that sorely needed one. The plan was for the students to have a life-changing experience—one that their parents paid $3,000 for and that might be useful in a college admissions essay—before going on safari and then heading home.

These kinds of expeditions are nicknamed "voluntourism" and, most likely, you have either been on a trip like this or know someone who has. On the face of it, voluntourism might look like a good thing: People like to travel *and* they want to create a positive impact in the world—so why not combine the two? Truth is, these trips are more than a little bit tricky ethically.

By day, Pippa and her classmates mixed cement and laid bricks, one at a time, to build the library. That task may sound easy enough, but Pippa could tell their skills were terrible. All the students found it challenging to straighten the bricks, and mortar oozed everywhere as they worked. One day, Pippa skipped lunch to speak with one of the local workers and ask for tips, because she saw that he was making progress at twice their speed. After lunch, she got back to work, determined not to be a total failure at her first building project.

The next morning, Pippa woke up at dawn, long before the rest of her tired-out classmates; she's always been an early riser, and the jet lag didn't help. To pass some time, she went for a run around the compound where they were staying and where the new library would stand. She didn't get far before she stopped in her tracks. There were the local workers, redoing the structurally unsound bricks the students had laid the day before. They worked silently, with no equipment, so as not to wake the students and make them aware of their failure. It hit Pippa like, well, a ton of bricks: This trip was just a charade to bolster privileged kids' college applications. She wasn't making any real impact on the community. In fact, this voluntourism experience was creating *more* work for the people there.

Years later, Pippa wrote a viral blog post about the experience. Through research and her own introspection, she concluded that what drives people to travel elsewhere to fix problems is actually the broken parts of their own lives. They're unfulfilled by a job that helps the rich get richer, jaded by indulgences that could be better spent saving a life elsewhere in the world. "We are seeking out entertainment and fulfillment from somewhere else. In any other case, we'd call it running from something," Pippa says. "But because it's socially recognized as 'good,' we say it's running toward something, to a higher calling."

Welcome to the bottom left corner of the action matrix, the realm of Misguided Moves. These are actions that make a single situation worse for others, and they are symptoms of a larger systemic failing, like colonialism or racism (or a combination). The outcomes of Misguided Moves run the gamut from frustrating and a waste of resources, as the workers on Pippa's service trip faced, to dangerous, as Marta experienced. Many Misguided Moves are simply ineffective; food kitchens, for example, have long asked the public to donate money instead of cans from the back of our pantries. In 2011, NPR ran a story with the founding executive director of University of Pennsylvania's Center for High Impact Philanthropy, Katherina Rosqueta, in which she noted that donors can feed twenty times more families by providing the same amount of cash you would've spent on a box of cans. Food kitchens have access to highly discounted food, so your cash would go much further with them than at your supermarket. Yet every Thanksgiving, boxes and boxes of canned goods show up without fail.

As you continue learning, resist the urge to judge others who have made mistakes that they later realized did not line up with their values. Keep your focus on relentlessly assessing your *own* motives and work. One way we keep ourselves honest is by looking back on our early work and evaluating where we have failed and what we do differently now.

For example, Tammy dug up emails she sent on behalf of She's the First and blog posts she wrote when the organization was just getting off the ground. Reading them now, she winces and cannot believe that, ten years ago, she was a perpetrator of the very system she is a critic of today.

In 2010, Tammy had a Peruvian friend who lived in the United States. Her friend had gotten involved with our earliest She's the First fundraising endeavor, a benefit concert, back when STF was still more of a fundraising machine for girls' education than a well-rounded nonprofit. Tammy's friend suggested she join her on a trip to Peru, where they could stay with her friend's aunt, squeeze in a sightseeing trip to Machu Picchu—one of the seven Wonders of the World—and visit orphanages to find programs She's the First might be able to support. *Brilliant idea!* Tammy thought, *Let's turn this into a bigger project!* She called it "STF 360" and described it: "Voluntourism meets digital storytelling in She's the First 360. We're building a user-generated travel series where young people visit the partners in the She's the First directory, talk to locals, and capture the stories of their girls and community through video, photography, blogging, and social media. We piloted the series this August with a trip visiting nonprofits and orphanages in Peru."

Tammy was working by day as a website editor for *Seventeen* magazine. You can probably see how her work at a magazine directly influenced her ideas—creating user-generated content as opposed to what a community actually needed. None of the fundraising She's the First was doing went to the nonprofits and orphanages she visited in Peru: What could possibly have been in it for *them?* Just the hope that money *might* come from these intrepid Americans?

On this journey, Tammy and her friend taught five classes at a school to students with challenging backgrounds. An exercise prompted the students to reflect on what they would be the first to do and what kind of goals and dreams they had for their future. Tammy later blogged: "We couldn't have asked for a better way to end #STF360 Peru than asking girls to interpret our mission and meaning for their own lives. It was an honor—and only the beginning of She's the First going global." Today, she would never approach a situation asking girls to "interpret" our mission—She's the First would put in the work to find out what girls ask of *us* and the adults in their communities.

Although there is value in classroom activities that get girls (and boys) dreaming about their futures, without investing in programs that will help them *achieve* those goals, how useful is it for a few outsiders to pop in for a day? To go back home to safety and support, capturing one heartfelt story for their own blogs, while those students face a different reality, lacking access to resources and programs that will move them forward?

On other parts of the trip, they toured three orphanages. Tammy, the college journalism graduate, blogged about how they operated and what they needed. The thing is, in her mind, she was making all the right moves. In one blog post, Tammy wrote, "If you want to do good, first listen to the people you want to help. . . . That's what She's the First 360 is all about—asking questions to understand need." That's one of the core principles of this book, so even a young and naive Tammy got something right. But after a decade of working inside a nonprofit and hosting visitors herself on international trips, Tammy now knows that flying thousands of miles from home to ask questions is not efficient if it costs local organizations more than it gives in return.

Misguided Moves don't have to be dramatic or tragic; many are much more subtle. They can take busy leaders away from people who desperately need them, simply for your own edification and fulfillment. They can reinforce a negative stereotype or narrative, which undermines the empowering work you're trying to do. The effects of that may be overwhelmingly positive for you, fueling you to do great work in the long term, but it's still negative for someone on the receiving end of your actions if they don't have anything of equal or greater benefit to gain.

Today, the two of us are conscious of not burdening those who have even fewer resources than we do. We encourage others to likewise be mindful of not putting their needs ahead of the girls we serve. If Tammy could do it all over again, she'd scratch the concept of STF 360 entirely, and if she wanted to go on a learning trip, she would first fund-raise a significant amount of money for the places she, an untrained volunteer, was visiting. If she wanted to be a reporter, she'd do so for a news outlet with an audience big enough to change attitudes and behavior versus a tiny blog. Or she'd simply take a trip to experience the foods, culture, and fun of a place elsewhere in the world, meeting as many people as she could along the way, and working to understand the nuances of a community different from her own.

You may have received mixed messages about voluntourism in the past, because some small global nonprofits, not ready to navigate the power dynamics with donors, do invite volunteers in hopes they'll become passionate and raise much-needed funds. In the best-case scenario, that does happen. In the most harmful scenario, vulnerable children form attachments to each set of short-term volunteers and struggle to form secure attachments to others in adulthood. In many cases, the scales are simply tipped and weighted to the benefit of the visitor.

You can also recognize how voluntourism maps pretty neatly to the ideas that helped shape colonialism, in which white Europeans firmly believed they had a moral obligation to "help" African (or other Indigenous) people by telling them exactly what would be best for them, what they had to believe, and how to improve their societies. It upholds a worldview in which white people are the "saviors" of other groups, generally those of darker skin, showing them the "right" and "modern" way to live. This is where the stories of starving children in Africa, oppressive Muslim men, and uneducated South American children come from. The message many Americans hear, even today, is that if you are fortunate enough to have an education and money, then you're the person these people need to save them from themselves, regardless of your expertise. This same kind of principle and narrative applies across all kinds of identities: able-bodied people "saving" disabled people, men "protecting" women, and so on.

White saviorism has become the phrase to define the specific relationship that follows a history of colonialism, but the ethos applies across many social groups. It's worth understanding these issues, because after a decade of working in international development, we have to tell you: When it comes down to it, many methods of voluntourism support a system of oppression that sticks around much longer than its participants do.

This isn't to say that you should stay at home or only look to create impact locally. We believe in a global community, one in which we are all connected, and obviously, we have chosen to focus our own professional impact on an international scale. Please do travel if you're able. It's an incredible privilege and a way to better understand the world around you. Immersing yourself in other cultures, across your city or across the globe, allows you to confront your own biases and assumptions about other places and people. If you want to create impact elsewhere, travel there—but please, go as a tourist. Experience new places as a learner, a student, and not as a savior. Look for activities that will allow you to engage in cross-cultural connection, and look for programs that will show you their work in mutually beneficial ways that avoid a hero-victim dichotomy between visitors and program beneficiaries.

TRAVEL TEST

When considering a volunteer program abroad, use these questions to determine whether your good intentions will match the outcome.

1. Would you be qualified enough to provide the service you're about to provide internationally if you were to instead do it within your own community?
   ☐ yes ☐ no ☐ not sure

2. Would it be acceptable for you to provide the service or attend a similar experience in your own community?
   ☐ yes ☐ no ☐ not sure

3. Look at the financial cost of your trip: Is the service you're providing worth more than that?
   ☐ yes ☐ no ☐ not sure

4. Is your role unable to be filled by a local community member?
   ☐ yes ☐ no ☐ not sure

Be honest with yourself. If you're checking off no more than yes, consider what you are hoping to get from this experience and whether you could achieve that outcome without leaving home. If you really just have the itch to travel, you can still scratch it! Just stick to tourism. Travelers help boost local economies, and this provides a way for you to forge cross-cultural connections while respecting local communities.

You don't have to travel for bias to show. A twenty-seven-year-old Floridian once saw photos of African children wearing tattered shirts—or none at all. So, he thought: *Why not collect one million shirts to ship over to Africa?* He had a T-shirt start-up and a closet full of shirts that he no longer needed. He launched his campaign with a simple website and YouTube video called "1MillionShirts.org: Trying to Donate 1,000,000 T-Shirts to Africa."

It didn't take long for foreign-aid bloggers and people who actually lived in African communities to tear his campaign to pieces. In short, they detected a Misguided Move. This guy had never visited Africa, never worked on an aid project, and didn't show any understanding of the fact that Africa is actually a diverse continent with a positive-growth economy. The cost of shipping a million T-shirts to an African country, when a shipping container alone can run thousands of dollars, raises the question of how that money could be better spent if local leaders and NGOs were to assess a community's needs and decide.

Toms Shoes faced a similar obstacle when trying to create impact through a one-to-one business model. For every pair of shoes a customer bought, Toms donated a pair to a child living in poverty. After receiving criticism and then commissioning studies to assess its impact, Toms pivoted by shifting a third of its production to create jobs in the communities where it did shoe drops. And now, other products of the brand, like sunglasses, coffee, bags, and backpacks, donate a portion of proceeds to impact grants that contribute to ending gun violence, homelessness, and gender inequality, as well as to sight restoration and safe water systems. The cash is more useful to changemakers than the reciprocal products. Those specific items might not be what people really need, even if they do give American customers that little burst of do-gooder dopamine and help a company sell more goods. Toms turned a Misguided Move into a Systems Solution (our favorite quadrant, which we'll dive into soon!).

In social entrepreneurship, many innovative ideas seem brilliant at first pitch and quickly build momentum without proof of concept. One of the most popular climate projects in recent history has been the engineering and building of a gizmo to clean up the Great Pacific Garbage Patch. This area is the largest accumulation of ocean plastic in the world, and it's located between Hawaii and California. In 2012, the then eighteen-year-old founder of the Ocean Cleanup project did a TEDx Talk about his idea that went viral. He got serious airtime because his product sounds like a dream: It's energy-neutral and very science-y, and he shared lots of charts, graphs, and studies for how this system of buoys was going to save our oceans. A crowdfunding page raised millions, followed by investments from the Dutch government and the CEO of Salesforce.

The only problem? Not *one* scientist has signed off on it. In fact, a group of scientists have dedicated research time to a peer review of the project's feasibility study in an effort to encourage the project's redirection. As the scientists went on to point out, this $35 million project will be *completely ineffective* at its job. Turns out, the project is meant to collect any garbage floating up to five meters below the ocean's surface. Unfortunately, almost all of the ocean's plastic ends up shredded into pieces of microplastic that sit on the ocean floor, more than thirty-six hundred meters below the surface, where marine life feasts. The project *looks* like a great idea because it's addressing an issue we can *see*, and it was fueled by youthful passion, but it ignores the larger systemic issue of how so much plastic gets in our oceans in the first place. The project ends up misdirecting millions of dollars into an idea that simply won't work.

Another invention that scored creativity points and more than $60 million in funding from high-profile donors was the PlayPump, a technology that was supposed to bring drinking water to thousands of African communities. As children play on a merry-go-round-like device, water pumps from below the ground. You can almost hear the squeals of children's laughter and see the smiles of happy mothers as you picture it. Nearly seven hundred PlayPumps were installed across South Africa with plans for expansion across the African continent.

Today, this project is a famous failure in international development. It turns out the root problem in these communities was often water scarcity, so the PlayPump was useless if there wasn't enough high-quality groundwater close to the surface. Second, though the idea of collecting water as a by-product of children playing is a joyful one, put yourself in their shoes: *Would you want to run around a playground every time you needed water for a meal or bath?*

These creative projects that were meant to be Band-Aids actually turned into Misguided Moves because they failed to produce the intended positive effects. Instead of mitigating an unfavorable condition, they made things worse and wasted precious resources. Both the Play-Pump and the plastic catcher gadget raised (and squandered) a hundred million dollars between them. We can't help lamenting how these funds were misused; they are sorely needed in effective humanitarian and environmental projects elsewhere.

Other Misguided Moves just end up looking like, and serving as, a mound of garbage. After earthquakes, tsunamis, or fires, people feel compelled to help those who have lost everything. The only problem? Aid workers refer to the massive piles of donations given in such circumstances to be a second disaster because they don't have time to sort through the clothing, stuffed animals, and other detritus. Often, donors don't stop to think or learn about what's actually needed, so areas experiencing devastation end up with mountains of objects no one really needs.

Scott Simon of NPR did a story on this precise issue and spoke with Juanita Rilling, former director of the Center for International Disaster Information in Washington, DC. She told him, "The thinking is that these people have lost everything, so they must *need* everything. So people *send* everything. People have donated prom gowns and wigs and tiger costumes and pumpkins and frostbite cream to Rwanda, and used teabags, 'cause you can always get another cup of tea."

The intention to send clothing, toys, and other items to people in need is good—great, even—but the *impact*? Not so much. To avoid sending materials an organization or town won't or can't use, always look to see what relief centers or food kitchens are requesting. That will guide your donations to be more impactful; and if you can, giving cash never fails in helping with a disaster. Just as your Impact Plan finds the sweet spot where your own resources and skills meet what the world needs, be sure to research what is needed before you unload your goods. That way, you'll find the place where it can create true impact (and not end up rotting on a beach half a world away).

The best any of us can do is to commit to a growth mindset, never stop questioning ourselves, invite constructive feedback, and then really listen to it, even if it makes us uncomfortable. When we do that, we can correct missteps before they turn into a major setback.

The greatest success of the 1MillionShirts campaign is that it stopped before it truly started with its shipments—as a result of public derision, it became a learning experience for all, instead of a disaster. It is important to keep thinking of new solutions to the problems communities face, but then test them before fully investing. We should give promising ideas seed money for pilot testing and research, especially when they're locally sourced solutions.

AVOIDING A MISGUIDED MOVE

1. Remember to check in with experts, organizations, or organizers to determine what is most needed from supporters.
2. When setting out with your own project, be sure to talk to those who would be interacting with it most often. Stay curious. What do they think?
3. Adapt. If you learn that your actions turned into Misguided Moves, acknowledge the misstep, take responsibility, and pivot to find a solution that works.

SYSTEMS FAILURES

Returning to the matrix, let's shift to the lower right quadrant: Systems Failures. This one's a biggie. See, the most detrimental mistakes rarely belong to one person or one well-meaning group. Those mistakes are symptoms of bigger Systems Failures. These Systems Failures are rooted in policies caused by imbalances of political power and governance built on racism and bigotry. They are often justified by "good intentions" or "tradition" and cover up beliefs that people of different races, ethnicities, genders, and sexual orientations are not equal, need "saving," or require protection.

For one enraging, heartbreaking example, look at the border crisis in the United States during the Trump administration. In 2018, the Trump administration announced a "zero tolerance" policy toward migrants coming across the Mexican border into the United States. All undocumented adults crossing the border would face criminal prosecution and be placed in federal custody, even if they were traveling with children. Children would be separated from their parents and then face nightmarish conditions, trapped in cages at detention centers, with little or no access to showers, toothbrushes, clean clothes, beds, blankets, or enough food. It's not entirely clear how many thousands of children the US government has separated from their parents, but estimates start at 5,600 and run north of 60,000. In 2019, the Trump administration announced it would take up to two years to identify the thousands of children being held and reunite them with their families. *Two years!* Even after reuniting with parents, children face long-term damage, with trauma that makes them angry, withdrawn, and fearful that someone will take them away from their families again.

This is a Systems Failure because there are big powers at play: governmental policy, xenophobia, political polarization. It's common for a Systems Failure to have multiple causes or to trace directly back to a system of discrimination; for example, you can trace the pay gap Black women face directly back to racism and sexism. You can trace the low sentencing rates for rapists back to our system of patriarchy, where men made rules with men's needs in mind.

One of the difficult parts of Systems Failures is that it's easy to be complicit in them because you have little power individually to change them. Your ticket to a Marvel movie and takeout from Taco Bell could help fund some of them without you ever knowing it. (Both companies have leaders who donate to Trump and pro-Trump super PACs that seek to "Make America Great Again" by pulling out of climate accords in favor of corporate profit, normalizing bigotry, and slashing governmental aid for Americans most in need.) When you notice that you make slightly more than a coworker of another race for the same position, and you don't say anything? You've become complicit in corporate pay inequality.

The systems handed to us by the previous generation are broken and breaking, and they need to be fixed, but your actions aren't going to move the needle on their own. Collective action is so incredibly important, whether through voting or community organizing, and it's the only way we can attempt to reconfigure some of these failing systems to work *for* people instead of against.

Identifying Systems Failures is crucial so that you can identify where a problem is coming from and turn your collective action efforts in that direction. If you look hard enough, you might even spot a Systems Solution.

SYSTEMS SOLUTIONS

Here's where your spirits—we hope—will lift. We've now reached our favorite part of the matrix: Systems Solutions. Systems Solutions tackle the big, thorny, underlying problems in our society (or the problems within smaller systems, like a work sector or a community). You can contribute to Systems Solutions with actions that address the root of problems by changing policies and norms. Either you have the power or privilege to modify a system for the better, or you engage in collective action to get the job done. This is where you can realize the full potential of your Impact Plan.

Remember Veronika, who was distributing sleeping bag coats to people facing homelessness in Detroit? One day, a woman at the shelter confronted her with a massive truth: "I don't need a coat!" she shouted. Everyone nearby stopped what they were doing and the whole room got silent. "I need a job!" Her voice boomed as she repeated herself. She was fed up with Veronika, who at that point had been making many well-intentioned trips to the shelter to investigate how best to help people experiencing homelessness.

Veronika recalls the moment vividly. "I was caught off guard that my existence in this place had caused her that much anger," she said. Another person had to come over to deescalate the situation as Veronika walked out, completely defeated. That day, however, Veronika came to understand the difference between a Band-Aid and a Systems Solution. And it didn't take long until she knew that woman who was at the end of her rope was right. She couldn't stop at treating the symptoms of poverty with a coat; employment opportunities had to break the cycle of poverty and prevent the need in the first place. If she could do that, then she'd be contributing to a Systems Solution.

Veronika turned her coat manufacturing into a nonprofit called the Empowerment Plan, whose mission is to permanently elevate families from the generational cycle of homelessness. To do that, they hire single parents from local shelters and provide them with training and full-time employment as seamstresses so they can earn a stable income, find secure housing, and regain their independence. Part of their workweek includes supportive services that address their needs pertaining to education (like studying for a GED), housing, childcare, and transportation. It's been a huge success. Employees usually graduate from the program after two years and get jobs at larger companies, and no one has fallen back into homelessness since the program began in 2012.

In the United States at large, we suffer from a warped, broken system of racial injustice, tracing back to the days of slavery, the very origins of our country, and before then, to the ways of colonizers. Fixing that requires a total dismantling of society and a rebuilding. That sounds impossible, but bear with us here.

Because Band-Aids don't heal the wounds created by unequal systems, long term, we need Systems Solutions, which often require the combined efforts of many people and take time. Gradually, real change happens. You see that change reflected in policy, stronger economies, or more accepting social behaviors. You can contribute to a Systems Solution any time you take actions that lead to lasting change across an entire system.

On Christen's first trip to Uganda for She's the First, a few students invited her to their homes to share a meal and their experiences. One such student was the ever-smiling Justine, then in her last year of primary school. Christen walked home with her after school and met her parents and a few siblings. Justine's home was a place of warmth. They lived close to the local school and were happy to stand by the road and chat with friends and neighbors as they passed by. They extended that same warmth and friendliness to Christen, who immediately felt right at home. They were so proud of Justine, who was the oldest and the first girl in her family to head to secondary school.

Two years later, Christen was back in Uganda on a site visit. She stopped by the secondary school that Justine was now attending, but she didn't see her. She began asking around for Justine. The girls were quick to tell her that Justine had gone home, but they didn't say why.

Christen would later hear the truth from the school principal. Justine was pregnant at fourteen and had been kicked out. The thinking was that her presence in class would be a bad example for other girls.

She's the First would not give up on Justine. We started making calls. We learned Justine was at home with her parents, heavily pregnant by then. Christen worked with She's the First's local partner organization to sort through options for Justine after she had the baby: *Could they enroll her in a nearby school? Would there be someone who could watch the baby during the day? How could the community support Justine's needs?*

Eventually, after many discussions with Justine and her parents, the group settled on a plan: Through the rest of her pregnancy, Justine would live with a local teacher who could help her stay on top of her studies while she transitioned into motherhood. After giving birth, she'd return home, where her mother agreed to take care of the baby during the day. And after a few months, Justine would return to a new school, one she could easily reach from home.

Even this solution for Justine, as you might have identified by now, was a Band-Aid to a much bigger Systems Failure: Pregnant girls worldwide are often banned from school, which is a quick way to ensure girls never return and never graduate. Whether from shame, local tradition, or sheer exhaustion, teen mothers all around the world—including in higher-income nations in the Global North—are statistically unlikely to return to school after having a baby. But this Band-Aid of getting Justine back to school can pave the way for larger Systems Solutions by challenging our social response to teens who get pregnant.

Globally, a switch flips in the minds of communities whenever a girl gets pregnant. Typically, at fourteen, fifteen, sixteen years old, a girl is considered a child, with all the rights we bestow on childhood. If that same girl has a baby? She is now a mother and, therefore, an adult. Why do we no longer consider her to be a child? Her reproductive status has not changed her age; it has not changed her *right* to an education.

So, at She's the First, we began looking for solutions within our own systems regarding teen pregnancy. We now implement training programs in sexual and reproductive health and rights, and we host policy discussions for girls' programs, including how to incorporate the voices of girls in the decision-making process. We bring in local experts and girls themselves to work with partners on crafting policies and programs that fit the local culture while emphasizing girls' educational rights. These initiatives won't change the global system, but for the system we operate within, they drive a conversation that lifts up *all* girls. Meanwhile, we publish advocacy videos and messages, in partnership with local organizations, to shift attitudes about pregnant girls and work toward a larger Systems Solution.

Changing a narrative is one way to contribute to a Systems Solution, and you can incorporate that in your Impact Plan. Almost all Systems Failures have roots in cultural norms and attitudes. If you spot one that holds people back and is unjust, address it. Whether through writing opinion pieces, attending marches, or holding conversations with your own family, you can influence how people see the world. Public opinion is a huge impetus behind system transformation.

When Billy Porter became the first openly gay Black man to win a Primetime Emmy Award for outstanding lead actor in a drama series for his role on the TV show *Pose*, he used his acceptance speech to make this point. He highlighted the role artists can play in altering biased thoughts and behaviors, in his case about LGBTQ+ people. "It took many years of vomiting up all the filth that I had been taught about myself, and halfway believed, before I could walk around this Earth like I had the right to be here," he said. "We as artists are the people that get to change the molecular structure of the hearts and minds of the people who live on this planet. Please don't ever stop doing that." Public expression—television, movies, paintings, books, writings—can, over time, change cultural narratives.

At this stage, you can look back at your Impact Plan with a fresh perspective. Why have we explored this matrix here and in the last chapter? Because it's vital to understand how our actions land in relation to their positive–negative effects over time. The exercise helps us to (1) stay accountable to what works and (2) prevent our intent from leading us astray. Impact happens when we combine the Band-Aid approach (the actions we can take *right now* to triage the world's worst problems) with our contributions to Systems Solutions, which allow for the entire landscape to improve.

Refer back to the actions you've listed on your Impact Plan and take a tally: *How many contribute to Systems Solutions?* You'll want to have at least a few that are part of a movement to drive a system to change. Many issues are much, much larger than our ability to personally change them: toxic capitalism, patriarchy, racial injustice. These are not systems that one individual can dismantle. But we can work with others to build better, healthier systems, and so Systems Solutions work will often appear on your Impact Plan in the form of political involvement, community organizing, or other large-scale group work.

As noted earlier, it's expected that most of your actions will lean toward the Band-Aid corner of the matrix. That's okay! The goal of your Impact Plan is to make your personal legacy net positive. You're limited in the change you (or any of us) can create on an individual level, compared to what we can do together in groups. In the interim, you can ensure that your own actions are working toward a greater good, in ways small (Band-Aids) and large (Systems Solutions).

For a practical example, apply this lens to your volunteer opportunities to make sure the value you bring is sustainable. In Part I, you considered the skill sets you have to offer. Often, the most in-demand skills for smaller organizations are the back-office ones: organizing spreadsheets or Google Docs, setting up accounting software, creating data projections, or designing graphics for an upcoming campaign. The places organizations least need outsiders? The glorified or most visible ones: the teaching positions, the orphanage volunteers, the bricklayers. It's a different story entirely if you have a degree in teaching English as a second language or in child psychology or in architecture or construction, but for most of us, we shouldn't be standing in front of a classroom teaching second graders to read unless we are, you know, *qualified* to teach second graders to read.

So, think about the training and skills you *do* have. What could you teach or build or do? That's the skill you want to take with you into volunteering opportunities. As for making it sustainable? The best way to do that is to ensure that the people working on the issue full-time can continue the work. So, if you're able to teach a class on project management, graphic design, or photography, consider teaching the staff rather than program participants. Leave behind a guidebook or tool kit. If they're able to continue training others year after year, your impact will be exponential—and now, you're no longer talking about a Band-Aid fix, but rather a micro Systems Solution.

When we take or condone actions that slip under the x-axis into the land of Misguided Moves and Systems Failures, that's when we need to own up to the reality that our intentions misfired. When we don't work alongside communities, or support organizations that do, the unintended consequences are harmful. The best thing you can do when you fail is to immediately be accountable, recognize that you have work to do, and even ask, "How can I make this right?" For Pippa, making it right meant opening up an educational discourse and shining a spotlight on the murky ethics of voluntourism projects. To excuse blame and instead focus on good intent makes the conversation about *us*, the privileged ones, rather than about those with less power, who have been oppressed by inequitable systems.

THE QUICK TEST

Here's a handy tool to take with you. To increase the odds of your project succeeding, try asking yourself these questions:

Q—Are you **qualified**? If not, is there someone who can mentor and guide you as you learn?

U—Is what you're giving **unbalanced** with what you're getting? Our egos can trick us on this one. Weigh what you will get (being honest with yourself about social cachet, feeling heroic, Instagram likes, etc.) against what others will get from you.

Are the two at least balanced equally? Is there any way the imbalance could be favoring you? There's always a give and take; work to ensure you're giving at least as much as you're getting.

I—Have you **identified** where you have privilege and power in the situation, and what the consequences are for those who don't? If your plan doesn't work, who is most affected, and how?

C—Have you **consulted** the communities affected, or has the entity you're supporting done that? What do they have to say about the proposed plan or solution?

K—Do you **know** the root cause of the issue, and are you mitigating its painful symptoms, if not also preventing it from happening long term?

If the answers are no, don't give up! Just revisit the exercises in Part I to reassess what you do have to offer or how to find an Impact Partner more suited for it.

This part of the journey hasn't been easy, but we're so glad you've stuck with us. All the practical advice in the world won't matter unless strong ethics and philosophy underpin it. Now that we've given you plenty to think about, let's spend more time reconnecting with other changemakers, plotting out *who* you can keep talking with about these questions. The upcoming tools and strategies will help you continue doing work that matters—no matter how hard it gets.

Part III

PERSEVERANCE

chapter eight

ESTABLISHING A
SUPPORT NETWORK

THINK ABOUT THE most purpose-driven people you know. They seem to attract like-minded folks, don't they? Let's explore how to build and enhance the web of people who surround you on this journey. The right support network will inform, inspire, and motivate you to stay on track with your Impact Plan.

Creating impact, as Part II showed us, is about *outcomes*. *Accountability* means taking responsibility for the outcomes of our behaviors, choices, and actions. And the good news is, accountability is a skill, so there are ways to practice and get better at it. Even if you are naturally disciplined, eventually you wear yourself down and need encouragement from the outside. As proven in the study mentioned in Chapter 4, other people keep you accountable to your goals, serving as motivators, collaborators, and mentors. But who, exactly, do you recruit?

Imagine you are hosting a dinner party. Picture a long dining table outside in a beautiful backyard with twinkling lights overhead. Plates, napkins, silverware, and glasses are carefully in place. Tall white candlesticks are lit. A vine of flowers runs down the table. You can invite ten guests (people you know or friends of friends) and, don't worry, anyone who doesn't make the cut will never find out. So, with no obligations and no pressure, choose the ten people with whom you want to talk about your true ambitions, including your impact goals. These are the friends and acquaintances who, when you leave their company, seem to put a spring in your step. They make you feel a little more invincible, push you to dream a little bigger, grow a little more, and they'd probably say you do the same for them. If only you could bottle up the energy you feel after hanging out with them to uncork on the tough days.

Our friend networks are multifaceted, ever the more so because social networks allow us to stay loosely in touch with people who, in any other era of human history, would have faded from our lives. Imagine if your dinner party, instead of being one intimate table, filled a football field with round tables, and you had to invite five hundred people you consider a past or present friend. You'd likely start categorizing these friends so that certain groups could sit together because of what they had in common: the "high school friends," "neighbor friends," "trivia team friends," "parenting friends," "writer friends," "work friends," and so forth. Certain friends are situational and only interact with a particular part of your life. That's fine, so long as they strengthen that part of who you are. Other friends rise to the top because they connect with you as a whole person, and they're friends not only with who you are now but also with the person you want to be. Those are the people you want to spend more time with!

Author and professor Geoffrey Greif has a catchy way of identifying four key types of friends—all of whom are important in different ways. He calls them your *Must, Trust, Rust,* and *Just* friends.

- *Must* friends are the ones with whom you are closest and the first ones you text when something big happens. They're your ride or die.

- *Trust* friends have integrity and earn your respect, but they aren't in your innermost circle yet. You feel like they could be if you spent more time together.
- *Rust* friends are old friends with whom you share personal history, like growing up together, but not a lot of current interests.
- And *Just* friends make for enjoyable company and chitchat, but you rarely see them outside of a specific context, such as in the office or at the dog park.

There's truth to those buckets, right? The two of us find that Must and Trust friends are *vital* to our Impact Plans and staying balanced; they are our rocks when we doubt ourselves. They are our mentors when we're in tough situations.

But these friendships don't just happen. Surrounding yourself with friends who make you the best version of yourself, rather than people who are stuck on a version of you that you've outgrown, takes intentional and proactive effort. It's easy to default on the friends you've known for ages or who are closest in proximity, like coworkers. We're all busy, and routines and social pressures work hard to keep you with your same friends, doing the same thing. But it's really important to question those relationships to see whether they're supporting who you want to become. Aminatou Sow and Ann Friedman, best friends, authors, and cohosts of the Call Your Girlfriend podcast, define the relationships we're after by the Shine Theory, a practice of mutual investment in each other and being collaborators rather than competitors.

While we worship Shine Theory now, the two of us didn't always get it right. In our early years working together as twenty-somethings, we both had insecurities about our leadership that made us protective of our respective domains and who got credit for what. Christen wasn't interested in Tammy interacting with our global partners; Tammy wouldn't loop Christen into media interviews; and we weren't lifting up the other's achievements in board meetings or at large. Neither of us felt animosity toward the other, but we each nursed the insecure voices at the back of our brains insisting that to be the best leader, we needed to showcase our own strengths. That defensiveness and low-key competition actively hampered our ability to thrive either together or separately. Shine Theory is all about an abundance mindset; it's based on the idea that the wins of those around you lift you up, too, and that supporting others will ultimately allow you to live a more connected and successful life.

Through the years, we opened up to one another about those insecurities, and like magic, we were able to banish them—together. When we talk about being "work wives" now, what we mean is that we actively worked on our relationship to arrive at a place of mutual understanding, support, and joy in collaborating. We realized we each become more successful, personally and with our goals for She's the First, when we make the time to "glow up" the other, whether by sharing her wins externally, helping her prepare for a big-stakes meeting, or being the cheerleader when she's hit a wall. If your closest relationships aren't aligning with Shine Theory, you don't have to write them off: Try working with that person to arrive at a place where you both feel supported. Investing in the relationships you have with people who invest in you is incredibly important to life and to your work in impact.

Aminatou, who created Shine Theory with Ann, underscores the importance of this. She says, "The people we bring into our lives actually help shape our future. Even if it's not happening explicitly, friends are always influencing the direction our lives take. Our own tastes, opinions, and desires have been heavily influenced by each other. And so of course we want friendships that feed and support our big, long-term goals! We want friends who help us set bold goals and look forward, rather than friends who subtly nudge us to make ourselves smaller."

Our Must and Trust friends light up our lives by cheering us on, empathizing with us, and helping us plot ways forward when we get stuck. They fuel us. If we let life get in the way, months could go by before we hang out with our most uplifting friends! So we look for routine ways we can make sure we are getting their dose of encouragement and positivity. For instance, Tammy seeks out free fitness opportunities and invites a different "dream dinner party" friend along with her most weeks, and then catches up over coffee after. (It's also a sneaky way to hold herself accountable to her wellness goals.) Christen loves to cook and loves to eat, so she builds her Must and Trust friendships over food or coffee and is especially fond of bringing new people together. It's rewarding to watch your own friends connect and find ways to lift each other up, knowing you were the matchmaker.

We have seen other people unite their friends in giving circles, like a group of women in New Jersey who meet for an annual "May Day" brunch and everyone chips in what they can, from $50 to $500, and collectively they make a larger gift to an organization they want to impact together. One Impact Planner, Michelle, hosted a "postcard picnic" over the summer, where she invited friends to meet her in the park for catching up *and* civic volunteering. She brought cards, markers, stamps, and snacks so that in between conversations about work and life, they could write postcards for the American Civil Liberties Union (ACLU) to mail out to districts that needed higher voter turnout.

Like Michelle and the May Day Women, we're drawn to people who are looking for ways to underline an activity they'd be doing anyway, such as sitting in the park on a sunny day or having brunch, with an extra layer of purpose. These people don't need to have the same North Star as we do. Sometimes they do; other times, our issues of concern intersect, and through their deep passion and knowledge in another area, we feel inspired, reenergized, and more informed.

If you're finding that you haven't based your friendships around a cause or your North Star, don't panic. Think of this like finding a gym buddy or a book club. Follow these steps to build up your network of peers:

1. **Start with who you know.** The more you talk to your current friends, the more you might find that they'll surprise you with their own passion for the same or a similar cause. Give them a chance to rise up and meet you for the journey.

2. **Sign up for a few cause-related happy hours or volunteer events hosted by local organizations or community groups.** Try meeting new people who draw energy from the causes you do.
3. **Connect online first.** Engaging people interested in your North Star will help you understand the issue better (more on that in a moment), and it can also lead you to great connections you can take offline to support your Impact Plan goals.

BRANCH OUT TO BUILD YOUR ADVISORY BOARD

Now imagine you could surround yourself with role models and leaders whose North Stars are similar to your own, people whom you could constantly learn from, who give you a new vocabulary that empowers you to talk about issues in compelling ways, and who could curate what you should read to stay informed. Above all, they'd keep you from feeling alone or insignificant in the fight.

What we're describing is an Impact Advisory Board, and it's available to you *right now*. You can build one and use it as your personal and secret tool. Your members don't even have to know that they're serving on it.

You've just looked at the kinds of friends you have in your life and some different ways to value these friendships. That's important, because you'll stretch yourself further knowing you've got their safety net of support. Not everyone needs to be a friend to play a part in your impact journey, though. They can be colleagues, partners, resources, or role models seen up close or from afar.

On your Impact Advisory Board, we encourage you to have the following types of people:

- **Supporters:** People who will back you (financially, emotionally, or otherwise) no matter what
- **Experts:** People who are knowledgeable authorities in your subject area

- **Leaders:** People who have skills to translate that knowledge into action
- **Firsthand advocates:** People with lived experience in the area, those who have been directly impacted by the issue you're looking to solve. Ideally, this includes yourself, as we've said—but if you're working on an issue that you're not directly served by or that you only know from a particular angle, you need to ensure you're surrounded by those who have been affected on even deeper levels.

Looking back at your "dream dinner party" guest list, you've got a base of supporters, particularly among your Must and Trust friends. From there, before you send off emails to subject-matter experts and leaders you don't know *quite* as well, our advice is to start where you already have a full-access pass: the internet.

ORGANIZING YOUR ACCESS TO EXPERTS, LEADERS, AND ADVOCATES

Conveniently, experts and leaders leave a trail of brilliant TED Talks, papers, articles, and social media posts from which you can learn. At the risk of sounding a bit Type A, let us share some ways we strive to build our own customized classrooms, by streamlining the voices we make time for online. We aren't always this organized, but setting up some structure in advance keeps us informed when life gets chaotic.

As you begin to build your board, start where 3.5 billion of us already spend a great deal of time: on social media. Chances are you already follow organizations (nonprofits, political campaigns and leaders, coalitions, companies) that care about the same issues as you do. But, if you're not, now is the time to curate them. If you need ideas, simply google *best [platform] accounts + [issue]*, like "best Instagram accounts + climate justice." Someone, somewhere has already published lists of who they think are the best. What organizations pop up on this search? Do you already follow them on social media platforms? Have you subscribed to their newsletters?

Personally, we try to avoid mindless "social scrolling" as much as we can. It is an expensive use of time with a low return of useful information. If you don't know what you're looking for, it's like going to the grocery store without a shopping list. You leave with the junk food you would have avoided had you planned what to do with fresh ingredients in advance.

All to say, we've found ways to navigate social media to optimize our time and walk away with valuable insights. It just takes a little planning and accountability, and it will set you up for success in the long run. The trick is being selective and separating out what you really want to hear from the rest of the noise. You can even set a timer for this work to keep you on task: When the timer chimes after fifteen or thirty minutes, get off the internet and get to work elsewhere.

Follow as many people as possible whose quality work ladders up to your North Star. Glance at their feeds: Does their communication style resonate with you? Are they sharing (mostly) meaningful content? Then go on a following spree! Every time you add someone, the platform will suggest similar users: See whether those interest you. Here, you're looking for those who fit into the profiles of an expert, leader, or firsthand advocate.

Consider adding relevant:

- Professors and scholars
- Founders/executive leaders of organizations and movements
- Nonprofits, coalitions, campaigns
- Elected officials
- Journalists
- Media publications
- Young activists (fresh voices are important!)

To identify the right guides, ask yourself:

- *What's their goal, and what are their values?*
- *How do they talk about what they do?*

- *What does "impact" seem to mean to them? Does it align with my ideas?*
- *Does their personal experience align with the impact they're working to create?*
- *Are they inclusive in their efforts? Whose voices do they feature?*

If you're a super-organizer, you can curate Twitter lists, Instagram collections, or Pinterest boards of the most moving quotes, infographics, or images. Put aside a binder to file articles and reflections in. You can also redirect your impact-oriented newsletters into an inbox folder you check regularly. Create places, online or off, to return to for inspiration and refueling when you're faced with obstacles. You'll end up with a catalog of well-worded thoughts, arguments, and ideas that will help you find your own words along the way. ✳7

When we're minimizing screen time or on the go, podcasts are our favorite place to learn from fellow experts and leaders who bring a different perspective than we have. Listening to a podcast episode takes longer than hitting "follow" or subscribing to a newsletter but is multitasking-friendly. Download and save pertinent episodes and listen to them when you're exercising, commuting to work, or have free time to pay attention. Christen uses them especially when cooking; it has the added benefit of giving her something new and interesting to discuss over dinner!

Jot down a few notes when you land on a helpful person or podcast: Who's giving fresh and eye-opening insights about your topic? Do they have a newsletter or website with useful information?

Any one of us could make a million excuses when it comes to keeping informed and seeking diverse voices to expand our perspectives. From work to school to caretaking and family obligations—those are all legitimate time sucks. Don't let them distract you from hidden pockets of time that are easily wasted, when you might be mindlessly scrolling or daydreaming. While you're in a long line at the post office or waiting alone at the doctor's office or airport, use those moments to pop open your Impact Twitter List, Impact Playlist, or Impact

Newsletters folder. Not *every* moment has to be used this preciously; when in the mood to consume media, just prioritize turning to these curated channels first.

As you add experts and higher-profile leaders to your Impact Advisory Board, it won't matter that they aren't accessible for one-to-one chats or direct communication. You've chosen them because they leave a trail of public teachings to learn from. As you engage in activities and groups aligned with your North Star, you'll meet new people for your Impact Advisory Board you *can* speak with, but in the meantime, a virtual Impact Advisory Board keeps you learning, growing, and engaged in your cause.

HANDING OVER THE MIC

Your Impact Advisory Board should consist of more than subject-matter experts; try to find people who have lived experience in your impact area, too. Even when you're working toward impact goals related to your own experience, this helps you expand your knowledge and understanding of the issue beyond how it impacted you personally. If the issue you're working on isn't directly grounded in your own experiences, this inclusion becomes even more crucial to your success. And in that case, you also want to listen to them and amplify their voices above your own.

Newer activists and changemakers often freeze when thinking about what to say about the issues they care about, online or in person. They don't want to screw up, misrepresent the issue, or say the wrong thing—and they definitely don't want to get called out for it. But being a changemaker doesn't require you to be the spokesperson for your cause. You can advocate for change by passing the mic to those who *are* ready to testify to the issues because of their own lived experiences.

Taking a step back and centering the voices of others is particularly important when you're coming from a place of privilege. It matters because, historically, the voices of the oppressed—those most affected by social ills—are passed over in favor of the privileged classes' solutions and quick fixes. The result? The poor stay poor, discrimination rests comfortably in its seat within capitalism, and nothing *really* changes.

When you created your Impact Plan, a big consideration for landing on your North Star was your own lived experience in that area. But all North Stars will impact people other than ourselves, and the only way to account for inclusive change is to talk and listen to those who are marginalized. Creating space for other voices will only strengthen your advocacy.

You could include a family member entrenched in the issue, a former professor, a neighbor, a friend, a colleague—anyone who brings lived experience and a fresh perspective and who will help hone your ideas. Such advisors will keep you accountable and will never allow you to assume you know what is the best solution for a problem you haven't experienced yourself.

At the 2019 World Pride Parade in New York City, Danish model Josephine Skriver participated in L'Oréal's "March for Me" campaign, riding on their rainbow float. Although she's straight, her family structure wasn't hetero: Her lesbian mother and gay father raised her. "I would be at events and sometimes meet young children with gay parents or family members that were a part of the community, and they couldn't understand why sometimes they got strange looks, got asked uncomfortable questions, or even bullied," Josephine says. She wanted them to see an inclusive world.

Acceptance of LGBTQ+ relationships is deeply personal to her, which is why she agreed to be on the parade float. "These are times when LGBTQ+ voices need some extra amplification in a world that is still too unforgiving," she says. And even though she knew the facts, she was still worried about being asked a question she couldn't answer. She decided to bring along her close friend and international hairstylist Brenton Kane Diallo, who does belong to the LGBTQ+ community. That way, she'd have a trusted resource, essentially an Impact Advisor, close at hand for moments of representation.

This is a great example of how our value does not come solely from what we say. Often, it comes from who you can bring to the table and into the conversation. You don't always have to be the one speaking on behalf of others; it can be so much more powerful to bring someone else up to the podium or into the meeting and hand over that metaphorical microphone.

In short, it is nonnegotiable that your Impact Advisory Board includes people who don't look like you, people who have lived experiences different from your own, and people who can bring their perspectives to change that needs to happen. Even if you have personally experienced problems in your area of impact, including others means you won't get too myopic about the issue.

DIVERSIFYING YOUR IMPACT ADVISORY BOARD

One reason we're so intentional about the diversity of our network and Impact Advisory Board is because it makes our thinking *better*, sharper, and more nuanced.

So, look back on your lists of experts, leaders, supporters, and organizations that might serve on your real or secret advisory board. Do a quick scan and note observations that come from the following questions:

1. Do you see different races, genders, generations, abilities, classes, and geographic areas represented?
2. Is there a mix of perspectives from the nonprofit sector, politics, activism, and academics?
3. Which categories of Impact Advisory Board members (personal connections, experts, or leaders) seem homogenous and could be more diverse?

Brainstorm how you could diversify, or go back to your online searches with an eye for including a broad range of voices into your thinking.

For your Impact Advisory Board, above all add people with credibility and vetted sources. Know that they won't always make you comfortable. Hopefully, they will expose blind spots of yours, requiring you to own up to mistakes you've made or revisit biases you have.

Speaking of voices that make us uncomfortable, we have one exception. We're sometimes asked whether to add people to your Impact Advisory Board who have values contrary to your own. For us, that's a hard pass. Nope! Different opinions create a rich tapestry for conversation; opposing values disintegrate productive conversation. That distinction is important; it *is* key to invite a difference of opinion to find the right way forward, but don't feel that you need to entertain the thoughts of someone who doesn't respect the same moral truths as you do. Besides, the experts and media we follow will likely respond to any notable opposing viewpoints, and that brings it to our attention. For instance, we're not interested in directly following anyone who doesn't believe the climate crisis is real or who doesn't take an intersectional approach to feminism. You only have so much energy; don't waste it on people with one-track minds or trolling behaviors.

A PEEK INTO OUR IMPACT ADVISORY BOARDS

Christen: My Go-To Girls

Because I spend so much time working on programs, trainings, and advocacy on girls' rights, it's critical for me to talk to girls. In my travels, I've met some incredibly insightful girls and women, whom I've gotten to know well over the past decade and who are, like me, very opinionated people. It works in my favor, though, because it means they're always there to give feedback and input on our programs and plans. In 2020, we turned that personal Impact Advisory Board into a professionalized Girls Advisory Council for the organization so we can institutionalize the inclusion of girls' voices in our decisions.

(continues)

I've also built up my advisory board with leaders of grassroots organizations (in the gender space and at large) who are available to talk through challenges, ideas, and new initiatives. Having these people in my life means I never make a programmatic decision in a vacuum, and following experts and leaders online means I can stay up to date on new ideas in the nonprofit and girls' rights spaces.

Tammy: My Mentors

I use the idea of an Impact Advisory Board both professionally and personally. Working full-time as a nonprofit CEO, I have a board of directors and am surrounded by people who keep me in tune with the most important ways to impact girls' lives.

I've long known what a tremendous asset a board was for She's the First, but it wasn't until recently that I realized I needed my own sounding board. I was connected to smart advisors who were helping us guide She's the First to maximum impact, but I couldn't always talk to them openly about my own trajectory. How could I continue to be the most impactful CEO of the organization I cofounded, while also dreaming of ways I could make an even bigger impact beyond that role?

That's when I called upon one of my personal mentors, Denise Restauri. Denise was vice president of national sales at *USA Today* for sixteen years, and then she launched a platform to amplify girls' voices. When I met her, she was producing the first-ever *Forbes* Women's Summit. Lucky for you, she also hosted a *Forbes* podcast called *Mentoring Moments*, where she interviewed changemakers who could be valuable to your own Impact Advisory Board. (Give it a listen!)

What makes Denise such a valuable member of my private Impact Advisory Board is that every time I bring a challenge to her, she's got a story to tell from her own experiences or about someone she knows. (Remember Jamira and Veronika, from our earlier chapters? Denise introduced me to both.) Most of all, Denise is someone who can see me doing more than I believe is possible. She's one of the first mentors who assured me that my future success and that of the organization I cofounded are not mutually exclusive. I could propel it forward from the outside, too. Denise has helped me see how I align my skill sets with ambitious opportunities while being truly happy.

INTEGRATING YOUR BOARD
INTO YOUR IMPACT PLAN

Hey, congratulations! You're well on your way to having your own Impact Advisory Board, and in your busiest moments, those advisors will keep you informed at a high level. Sometimes, you may message distant advisors and get a response. Other times, closer advisors will be mentors and friends you're lucky to call and meet up with any time you need. These are prime accountability partners, and we'll get to them in a second.

First, let's make sure you incorporate the work you've done in this chapter back into your Impact Plan. Check out your Easy Effort box. What goals did you set to stay informed on an issue? In what ways did you commit to nurturing a community?

Ideally, your goals are as specific, measurable, realistic, and inclusive as possible. Go back and see whether you could now update your plan with a little more precision. For instance, instead of writing "stay informed," you can say, "listen to a podcast from my Impact Playlist while at the gym each week." Instead of "follow climate experts on Twitter," you can say, "spend part of my lunch break scrolling through my Impact Lists; share an article or two I read on social media." Instead of "strengthen network," you could say, "plan a monthly coffee date with fellow volunteers."

You'll learn over time, and (if you're like us) over many cups of coffee, glasses of wine, and takeout containers, who your best collaborators are. Among the Impact Advisory Board members you regularly see and value, who really *gets* what you're doing? Who brings new insight or ideas to you about your work? Gloria Steinem hilariously titled one of her books *The Truth Will Set You Free, But First It Will Piss You Off!* In that vein, is there someone in your life who gets you riled up but ultimately is a truth-teller who helps advance your work and keep you on track? This person sounds like a great candidate for an accountability partner.

Accountability partners know what you want to achieve and check in regularly to make sure you're on the path to success. They won't let you blow off what you've said is important to you. As you look back over the lists you've made in this chapter, can you identify anyone you know who might serve as an accountability partner for you? Perhaps you can return the favor and be the same to them. (If you haven't guessed, we are for sure accountability partners to each other!)

BE YOUR OWN BOSS

As you continue to grow your network and find solid accountability partners, at the very least you can keep *yourself* accountable.

Out of necessity while growing She's the First, we developed the habit and mindset of treating ourselves like our own bosses. And technically, assuming we can experience our rights and freedoms, each one of us is the boss of our own life, so we might as well strive to be the best boss we ever had, right? That means being tough—holding *ourselves* accountable—but also being kind, supportive, and honest. Although we meet all the time to talk about She's the First's progress and needs, both of us individually schedule quarterly check-ins and evaluations with ourselves. We pick a place that brings us joy: the park, a cozy café, a rooftop or back porch space, our favorite spot on the couch, or maybe the window seat on a long flight. Bring a beverage, and make yourself comfortable and free of distractions. This can become a mid-year and end-of-year ritual rather than quarterly, but if possible, give it a try four times a year.

Think of your Impact Plan as being made of clay, not stone; you are shaping and refining it every time you check in. Be kind to yourself and be flexible. One Impact Planner, Marissa, learned this the hard way. Her North Star is a world where everyone has access to mental health care from well-trained providers in their own communities. After graduating summa cum laude from her undergraduate experience, she was at first rejected from the PhD program she had her heart set on. "It took me a while to learn that there can be many different ways to achieve a vision, because no matter how much you prepare, you can't control every outcome," she told us.

Marissa's initial rejection from a doctorate program led her to find a two-year job abroad as the volunteer and outreach coordinator for a school in Uganda. She then started grad school expecting to specialize in international work, but she discovered there was just as much need in the United States, in different ways. She recognized that choosing this path did not deviate from her pursuit of her North Star, so she reminds herself every time she checks in with her plan, "Let your vision evolve with you."

Another strong piece of advice we received on how to measure impact came from Kiersten Stewart, the director of public policy and advocacy you met in Chapter 2. "I always ask, what's your goal? Your impact is only measured by what your goal is." For example, Kiersten talks about comparing the impact of mobilizing a thousand people to send a letter to Congress versus inviting one general from the military to speak. Depending on the legislation she is trying to influence, the latter—engaging with one key person—could have more impact than reaching a thousand. Very much in the spirit of having an Impact Plan, she says, "Figure out your goal, figure out what the path to that goal is, and who is blocking that path. Are those the people you're trying to reach?" Or are you burning energy elsewhere?

Here's a fast way to take stock of where you are. First, start with your High Effort goals. If you're using our worksheet, strike through as many of the grayed tally marks, out of five, that show how far along you feel you are to completion. If you're creating your own sheet, pencil this in, in front of each goal. For example, at the moment of drafting this chapter, we felt we were four out of five tallies away from finishing our manuscript. (You're four out of five tallies from being done with this book!) This will give you a quick temperature on how fully baked your long-term projects are.

With your Medium and Easy Effort goals, you'll notice the Impact Plan worksheet has two checkboxes, one for a three-month check-in and one for your six-month check-in. Go down the list and leave marks in the relevant box:

☑ = you're on target, nailing it!
⌢ = you're doing it, sort of, but need adjustment or improvement
☒ = you hardly attempted this, if at all

We like to scan where we are before we reflect and strategize. If you're seeing lots of check marks, then you've been realistic with your bandwidth and accountable to yourself. Way to go! If you don't, and you're seeing lots of ~ and X, then you're still learning what's most important to you and where you're most effective or facing distractions you could mitigate. This is all valuable intel.

At each check-in, give yourself an assessment:

- Where am I seeing the check marks and why? Does this reflect what is most fulfilling to me—or is it simply what takes the least effort?
- What do I need to make more time for?
- What behaviors can I change to make the time?
- Where am I falling behind? Is this really important? Or am I better suited to do something else right now?
- Where can I, or should I, scale back?
- Have I started doing something purposeful that isn't here? Is it aligned with my North Star?
- What accommodations or support might I need to make these goals more achievable?

For goals you aren't hitting, make them less rigid and they might be more achievable between now and your next check-in. When you see double Xs in your boxes, though, maybe it's time to reconsider the importance of this goal to you. You might just be evolving in a different direction. Where you've got check marks, be proud! You could have been watching more Netflix shows or splurging extra cash on things you didn't need, but you chose another path and stuck to it.

To take stock of the tangible outcomes you created with your commitments, use the simple Progress Log template we've included in the workbook. ✳8 You can make this a running list on a separate page of your Impact Journal. The Progress Log reminds you to take a moment to appreciate what those check marks and tallies next to your goals mean. What are the results of your success? What are some wins that the purposeful groups you contribute to (nonprofits, political campaigns, boards, teams at work, etc.) have experienced?

The point of this reflection is to see that your efforts *do* add up and that you chose the right Impact Partners. It's common to obsess over falling back a step, just as it is to progress three steps forward without celebrating your achievement. On the days you face a setback and feel discouraged or insignificant, come back to this proof of your progress. If you choose an accountability partner, a written record of your outcomes will assist that person in helping you succeed further. You'll be glad you have it!

The real beauty of keeping yourself accountable on paper is that over time, you see you're not so scattered and insignificant after all. Your small actions *do* add up. What you prioritize is a telling sign of what matters most to you in the world, a glimmer of what you want your legacy to be.

chapter nine

BUILDING RESILIENCE AND GRIT

You may encounter many defeats, but
you must not be defeated.

—Maya Angelou

WE'D LIKE TO introduce you to the tardigrade. Imagine, if you will, a *very* plump, hairless mole. Now add three extra sets of legs, take away his eyes, and shrink him down in your mind's eye until he's just small enough that you can no longer see him and you need a low-power microscope to watch him wiggle. He looks like a super-tiny, overstuffed body pillow with legs.

Tardigrades are micro-animals that are sort of cute, depending on how well your microscope works. (Their nicknames are "water bear" and "moss piglet." Pretty adorable, no?)

The tardigrade is also the world's most resilient organism. These little guys can survive almost anything. They live in subzero temperatures in mud volcanoes on high-elevation mountaintops and in deep sea trenches. Scientists have subjected tardigrades to radiation, freezing, dehydration, starvation, and airless environments. Researchers even sent them off in a rocket and found that they *can survive in space*. Tardigrades just keep bouncing back, no matter how much pressure they're under.

And that's precisely why we're talking about them here. Creating change—to our habits, mindsets, and lives, as well as creating change in the world—takes *work*, and this work requires us to sharpen the twin skills of resilience and grit. Because these are skills, not fixed traits, we can constantly practice and improve them. *Resilience* is our ability to recover from failure or setbacks; *grit* is our motivation to keep going, the passion and perseverance for long-term meaningful goals. And it doesn't get more long-term and meaningful than your North Star, does it?

Without resilience and grit, or without our inner tardigrade, we'd quit before we got anywhere. It's just too easy to give up or give in otherwise.

As a changemaker, you show up every day, even when on most days, you aren't appreciated or recognized, you face rejection, and you can't see the payoff. When you're engaged in any type of justice work, you're inherently working against broken systems and structures, which is, by default, difficult, and trying to live within those oppressive systems is like trying to move a thousand-pound boulder that's pressing down on your heart and mind. Try as you will—with *all* of your might—to shift it ever so slightly, it just won't budge. Building your resilience and grit will help you keep at it . . . but how should you do that?

Athletes offer endless inspiration. Swimming champion Kristin Duquette knows about resilience and grit, as an American Paralympic record holder *and* social justice activist who just won't quit. She's been a competitive swimmer since the age of nine, right around the time she was diagnosed with muscular dystrophy, which causes progressive weakness and muscle loss. That didn't stop her from swimming, though; instead, she relied on the sport even more to strengthen her muscles without putting stress on her joints. Kristin's lifelong commitment to her goals, and her ability to work through physical, emotional, and external setbacks to achieve them, is exactly why we knew she'd have advice to share.

To give you a sense of what Kristin has accomplished as an athlete before the age of twenty-nine: She holds five American Paralympic records, is the former US team captain for the 2010 Greek Open Swimming Championships, and completed a Half Ironman open ocean swim.

When Kristin was training for the 2012 Paralympic Games in London, she realized that something was wrong with her right arm. Doctor after doctor dismissed her condition as a symptom of her muscular dystrophy, but she knew it wasn't. The hot and cold sensations and the shocks up and down her arm were not a standard sign of a progression, which usually happens gradually. When she finally found someone to treat the real issue, an irritated nerve in her neck, it was ten months later, and her dream of winning a medal was hanging on by a thread. She faced an intense road to catch up and get into top shape for trials.

Kristin knew it might not work out, but she still found the grit to keep training, two hours a day, six days a week, in addition to cross training. "I always want to look back on different periods of my life and know that I gave it my whole heart," she says. "I strive to not be held back by my inner doubts and fears, but instead wholeheartedly go for that goal or dream."

Ultimately, Kristin didn't make the team. But when your plans don't quite work out, Kristin reminds us that there is beauty and significance in the struggle. "Even if I don't understand why something didn't work out in the moment, I will see it in the future. Those moments are never wasted time."

Kristin's North Star is a world where social norms and systems work for humans and not vice versa. When she was done competing, she wanted to join another high-performing team, the Obama administration, and within a year, she was appointed confidential assistant to the chief of staff for the National Endowment for the Arts. She also speaks on disability rights at the UN and World Bank, encouraging audiences to imagine for themselves a world where disability is accepted as just another human experience. Kristin's resilience in the pool ultimately taught her to stay circumspect about challenges in other areas of her life, including her impact work.

"I used to feel really overwhelmed when it came to social change," Kristin says. "One of my role models is Nelson Mandela. I used to think that if I didn't become the next Nelson Mandela, my life wouldn't have much meaning. And that's so extreme and, quite frankly, an incredibly unhealthy mindset. Now, I believe so much change can happen collectively at a microlevel. The conversations I have with people, the words I choose, the way I approach my life can create change—and it's not up to me to judge the magnitude of anyone's impact. We each hold the power to unlock the resilience of the human spirit."

TESTING OUR OWN RESILIENCE

You never know what tomorrow brings, but if you're young, healthy, and living in a stable environment, you get comfortable in the status quo. You make plans that you can count on. The two of us experienced that steadiness through our entire decade working together. And then, as we put the finishing touches on this manuscript, everything changed. During a global pandemic, like you, we couldn't be sure if our elder family members, our colleagues, or either of us would be healthy the next day. We could not be sure how the impending recession would impact fundraising and our ability to sustain vital programming for She's the First. As hospitals overflowed, death tolls rose, and the economy faltered, we knew that the goals we had set for the year—and honestly, the next few years—had to fundamentally change. Our choices, and yours, too, were to succumb to the loss and scale back or pivot and move forward in our new reality.

Resilience is not a competition. How often have you compared your situation to others', thinking of someone who has it worse, and then comforting yourself that at least you don't have it "that bad"? An "if they can deal with that, I can do *this*" type mentality. It's valuable to find inspiration in others and to be grateful for what you have, but we've learned to avoid minimizing our own defeats or pain (or fetishizing the pain of others). Your obstacle is valid, no matter how it compares to someone else's. The same is true in reverse: Just as Kristin noted, your achievements don't have to compare to Nelson Mandela's or any other "famous" changemaker's to be valuable. What knocks each of us down varies widely, but the resilience it takes to get back up is what we have in common.

As human beings, our needs are more complex than those of our friendly tardigrade. We are not indestructible microorganisms. Unlike tardigrades, we have core psychological and emotional needs, and extreme weather (literal or otherwise) does affect us. We live and work in a culture that tells us to value hustling and productivity over all else. That means it's on us to prioritize our own well-being, through self-care, so we have the resilience not just to work hard but also to achieve outcomes that make a difference.

Ideally, you strengthen yourself for moments of disappointment, rejection, and failure before they happen, but if you haven't been proactive, it's never too late to start. Self-care was already a trending topic before it became an *absolute necessity* during social isolation in the COVID-19 crisis, when everyone's plans were upended.

THE CONCEPT OF SELF-CARE, surprise, surprise, made a resurgence during the 2016 election season and into the Trump presidency, when every single presidential tweet and news headline could make your blood pressure rise or stomach churn with fear. The commercialization of "self-care" into bubble baths, fancy candles, and face masks never clicked with us; these are soothing activities, but all this diluted what self-care means. Self-care isn't something that you can buy. Emotional intelligence writer Brianna Wiest put it brilliantly when she wrote, "True self-care is not salt baths and chocolate cake, it is making the choice to build a life you don't need to regularly escape from."

As entrepreneurs, the two of us were always, and still are, doing things we have never done before, so we often google "best practices" for the task at hand: best practices for hosting a staff retreat, building a board of directors, acknowledging donors, designing and evaluating programs—you name it. Best practices are the conditions that experts agree lead to the best results. So, then, what are the best practices for a life you wouldn't need to escape from?

When you have to leave a child or a pet, you give your sitter a whole rundown of what to expect from your precious little one, right? You want the sitter to understand all their quirks so that they'll be happy in someone else's care. As grown humans, we may not come with our own manual of best practices—the conditions in which we thrive—but we can surely create one. Most people, including ourselves, are rarely living by all of our best practices, all of the time. Regardless, you can still feel the effects of a strong, healthy life by doing most of them. In our experience, it's when you're feeling in a funk that you're probably *too* out of sync from your best practices.

We find three types of best practices contribute most to our resilience, and we bet you can relate.

1. BE KIND TO YOUR BODY AND BRAIN (AND CHALLENGE THEM EVERY NOW AND AGAIN)

You don't have to be a health expert to understand your body needs you to take care of it, and yet, look at how often we forget that. When we're stressed, we're more likely to overreact, spiral down the rabbit hole of worst-case scenarios, and thus feel helpless or lost. We're more likely to make bad decisions with how we spend our time and what we eat, and that affects our personal lives as well as our Impact Plans. When we get sufficient sleep and eat well, however, we keep our energy levels up. When we make time for exercise or learning new skills (physical or mental), we release endorphins that keep us feeling steady, balanced, and more prepared to take on the world.

This can be especially hard to remember when you're feeling sick, stressed, or otherwise overwhelmed. When Christen's endometriosis flared in 2018, her entire routine slowly fell apart: She was fatigued and could barely wake up in the morning, let alone make it to a boxing class; work was draining for her and she was too distracted by pain to focus in meetings; cooking dinner felt nowhere near as important as curling up in bed with a heating pad and some aspirin and waiting to see whether the pain would go away. The parts of her routine that normally gave her energy—exercise, work, good food—were suddenly burdens. And the rest of the activities she enjoyed, from sex to hiking to exploring new places? Forget it. Her new interests included pain alleviation techniques and Netflix.

As time wore on, this method of living wasn't going to cut it. As Christen accepted that her life was fundamentally changing, she began opening up to her partner, her friends, and her coworkers about her diagnosis and experiences with it. Their encouragement and support allowed her to look for ways to incorporate the things she loved in new ways: She signed up for a gym membership where she didn't have to show up at a specific class time, and she could go as easy or as hard as her body would allow. Her partner cooked dinners, which would draw her into the kitchen, too, even if just to keep him company. She started working from home more often, where her heating pad made it more tolerable to concentrate and do the work she loved most.

Finding these ways of adapting her routine to nourish her body and her brain was key to building the resilience she needed to manage her impact projects while dealing with a huge physical obstacle. Today, she relies on these same practices when she's stressed; you can still find her heading to the gym or taking advantage of the next tip.

2. BE MINDFUL OF WHO YOU SPEND TIME WITH, OFFLINE AND ONLINE

We touched on who you surround yourself with in Chapter 8. Those people increase your accountability and give you inspiration to go out into the world and do the right thing when it's not the easy thing. Recognize what and who makes you feel like the best version of yourself, who helps and motivates you, and say *yes* to activities with them. We all need and deserve care from others, and building resiliency is best done with the support of those who love us.

As you're assessing your community, also take time to recognize who the energy vampires are. What and who makes you feel depleted and snarky? Give yourself permission to avoid planning one-on-one time with them, or invite them to do something that changes the energy of the conversation, like running an errand or going for a walk instead of hanging out at the bar. Remember that you need to keep your cup as full as possible to continue achieving your goals and, ultimately, to create that positive legacy you want to leave. If something doesn't serve you or those goals, it's okay to say no!

Even those of us who are smart at how we spend our time with others in person still trip up over who and what we let into our life digitally. Set boundaries with the media that you're consuming to stay informed and in touch. For example, if you're prioritizing reading a couple newsletters, listening to a few weekly podcasts, and putting the morning news on for twenty minutes as you get ready, do you really need to be scrolling social media all day? Do you need 24/7 news commentary to rehash a disaster in a dozen different ways, or can you just take in the facts once and save your mental energy for constructive, creative, and solutions-oriented work?

3. SPEND TIME WITH YOURSELF TO TAKE YOUR STRESS OUT OF THE SHADOWS

How will you know what makes you feel good if you're not spending time with yourself to figure out what makes you click? Brain dumps are an effective way to curb anxiety and stress, because when you pour out what is bothering you on paper, it looks a lot less scary than it did when running around the dark alleys of your mind. When you can name your stress, it loses its power over you.

We both have a habit of exporting our anxieties out of our heads and into a journal we reserve for this purpose. If we're in the middle of something and a particular concern is nagging us, we jot it down on our respective pages. Christen dubs this space "the parking lot." When you write it down, it's like you're telling that concern, "I see you! Now pipe down. We'll talk soon." You park those thoughts until you're ready to let them take you for a spin.

When you have time to review your journal entries about what's bugging you (or exciting you!), you can more easily connect the dots on what isn't serving you and what's working. Usually, there's a direct connection for Christen between a lack of exercise or an abundance of high-sodium takeout and feeling groggy or tired. Tammy notices that her stress festers when she lets too much time pass between heart-to-heart coffee dates and phone calls with friends or allows work to override her exercise routine. Recognizing these patterns clues us in to the actions we can take to avoid defeat and burnout.

The hardest part about self-care is that, beyond a few guidelines, no one can *really* tell you exactly how to do it, because you have to listen to what your mind and body need—and no one knows that better than you. To find out, try spending small amounts of time alone, without the distraction of phone notifications. Take a walk or meditate; generally, see what feelings and emotions and ideas come up for you when you don't have messages, emails, or other people dictating what you'll think about next. Really listen to what your body and mind are telling you: What are you anxious about? Excited about? Does your body need rest, movement, water? Practice letting your mind and mood wander, until you better learn to take care of *you*.

PERSONAL BEST PRACTICES

Create a list of ten best practices that make you the strongest, most energized, and optimistic version of yourself. Here are several of ours, for example:

- Getting at least seven hours of sleep a night
- Working out or doing yoga multiple times a week
- Making time to journal and reflect on weekends

(continues)

- Scheduling out daily/weekly priorities in advance and time-blocking the calendar accordingly
- Using social media time for content creation (making posts) and limiting scrolling to ten minutes a day
- Taking a midday walk break or otherwise prioritizing time outside
- Having a catchup call or date with a friend or mentor each week
- Waking up with a cup of coffee and enough time to enjoy it

When you're starting to feel the energy vampires creeping around or the voices of doubt and discouragement in your mind, double-check that you're living up to most of your best practices, and adjust as needed.

Let's assume now that you're building resilience with a self-care routine that works for you, and you're living up to your personal best practices. Still, you'll stumble into obstacles and hard days. How do you keep that outlook from your best days on your worst ones?

Keiko Feldman, cofounder of Gender Nation, which donates LGBTQ+ inclusive books to school libraries, knows just how that feels. Building on the advice she gave us in Chapter 1, she has a practice for when she starts to feel pessimistic about her impact on the world. "There *are* days it's discouraging," she says. "We might put on a big fundraiser with celebrities and storytelling and, in the end, we make $15,000. It feels amazing in the moment . . . and then you actually spend the funds, and you realize, that wasn't nearly enough. You get the feeling that nothing you accomplish is good enough." Sound familiar? No matter how high you climb up the mountain, the top still seems so far away. But instead of focusing on how far she has to go, Keiko takes a deep breath and reassesses what she's done.

"I look back and reframe it. We donated packets of books, all of which are beautiful and uplifting and affirming and new, to almost a hundred schools, where they'll reach seventy thousand kids. And if I look at it that way, I can say, 'Wow. I did all that.' It's the same thing you do in everything—in nonprofit, in parenting, or your job. It's about mindset. You can look at it one way and think, *This is crap*. Or you can look at it another way and say, *Okay, this is good. Let's make plans to keep it going*."

"*Let's make plans to keep it going*" is maybe the simplest and most profound way to phrase the *how* of resilience when it comes to impact work (though *The Little Engine That Could* and her "I think I can, I think I can" mantra works just as well). Veronika Scott, in having the gaps in her homelessness project pointed out to her, could have easily thrown her hands up in the air and walked away or simply continued doing what she had been doing. But instead, she took stock and recognized that she had to factor in employment opportunities. *This is good. Let's make plans to keep it going*. Pivoting her plan didn't mean that the work she had done thus far was useless; it just meant that she was learning, growing, moving toward better outcomes.

The nature of impact work is such that, fairly routinely—especially as you start out—you are likely to make mistakes, misstep, and realize that your actions were not as meaningful as you might have hoped. The sheer size and the complexity of the problems you're tackling can often leave you feeling small and powerless. The world's problems can feel too big, too messy, with too many systems at play to address properly. You've probably sat and listened to someone say that they *know* their actions are just a drop in the bucket, so why limit their consumption or change behavior? The world is doomed anyway, and their single plastic straw will hardly be the one to break the camel's back.

And yet.

When you hear that argument, are you inspired to give up? Does it convince you that you should stop trying? Are you tempted to accept defeat and live life without intentionality or impact?

When you make plans to keep going, what you're ultimately doing is keeping hope, or optimism, alive. Hope is not enough to achieve a better world—it is powerless without systems change, tireless work, and collective action—but it is required to try.

In those difficult moments, here's how we keep our grit in high gear so we don't lose sight of our long-term goal.

1. STAY FOCUSED ON YOUR NORTH STAR

You need to pull motivation from *inside*, which is why finding the right North Star is so crucial. When the world gets tough, your North Star will motivate you to keep moving, with resilience and determination, toward your goal. The right North Star will pull you along through the mountains and valleys of changemaking, through your mistakes and missteps, your triumphs and victories, and keep you on track. That's why it's your North Star!

A big part of grit in the face of the world's problems is acknowledging how thorny these problems are and becoming comfortable living in that thorn bush, or at least tolerating the nicks and scratches. We won't see the long-term outcomes of our positive actions for decades. We might realize after five years that we ought to have done something differently. It's part of the process to accept this and to realize that we can't use the size of the problem or the stickiness of the issue as an excuse to stop trying. We can do *something*. Next time you're tempted to throw in the towel, when you feel small and inconsequential, think about those who are suffering most from the issue you're working on. Whereas it can feel easy to walk away from an abstract problem, it's much harder to think about facing a person and saying, *"I see you suffering, but it all seems too big and difficult, so I'll go back to brunch now. Good luck with that!"*

2. REJUVENATE WITH SMALL WINS

For both of us, it's not in our nature to rest on our laurels; after Tammy has a fundraising win or Christen pulls off another successful training program with our partner organizations, we're already trying to solve our next puzzle. We have to remind ourselves to celebrate not just the culmination of something we've worked on for months, if not years, but also the smaller victories along the way. When we do, we find that we walk away renewed with optimism, because it shows us that even if the world is getting tougher, so are we.

Think of how you can break your impact projects and goals down into smaller chunks. When you finish the task, treat yourself to a chocolate chip cookie from your favorite bakery, plan a relaxing movie night, or just sleep in the next morning.

Passion can lead us to do everything at once, and it keeps us focused on what remains to be done rather than on what we've accomplished. That's a recipe for exhaustion! Celebrating milestones forces us to slow down and appreciate progress, even if the end result is distant.

3. CHANNEL YOUR YOUNGER SELF

Young people are reservoirs of hope, perhaps because they haven't lived long enough to become cynical and see all the potential pitfalls. She's the First was born out of that youthful naivete. The older and more risk-averse we get, the more conscious we are about keeping alive the gutsiness that came naturally to us as teens and twenty-somethings. To their credit, our younger selves never considered throwing a benefit concert to be too audacious a task and didn't hesitate to ask friends' parents to support a worthy cause.

An easy way to keep this spirit alive is to surround yourself with younger people, and that's why mentorship is an activity that serves Impact Plans well. When sharing what you've learned the hard way with another person, you're also actively reminding yourself that you're more resilient than you realized.

AS WE WRAP UP OUR TRIBUTE to the humble, resilient tardigrade, there's one more connection worth noting between us, as changemakers, and this teeny creature: The tardigrade's resilience doesn't just benefit itself. As a pioneer species, it creates space for an entire ecosystem to thrive around it. Because they inhabit new spaces where few other creatures can survive, tardigrades pave the way for other organisms, who can feed off of them, to follow suit.

That's why we love the story of Ellie so much—she's proof of how one resilient changemaker with grit makes the way for another.

Remember how in Chapter 5, we told you about how she petitioned to change her university's policy so that she could be the first woman to run for student body president? She lost the election. And remember how she applied for a visa to visit the United States as an advocate? She was denied.

But that was hardly the end of Ellie's story. Two years later, after she had already graduated from university, another woman ran for student body president, inspired by Ellie's example. This time, with 80 percent of the vote, the female candidate *won*.

Around the same time, Ellie reapplied for a visa to the United States, once again to speak at a She's the First event in New York, this time for the International Day of the Girl. Back at the US embassy in Dar es Salaam, she waited in line, clutching her folder of paperwork to her chest once again. Waiting for her turn at the window, she noticed that one of the visa officers was a woman. *Please let me get the woman,* Ellie thought. One by one, Ellie saw the people ahead of her in line get rejected. When her turn was up, she heard a woman's voice: "Next!"

The officer looked over Ellie's papers, reading them closely enough to notice that she worked as a mentor and ran her own community organization. "How many girls do you mentor?" she asked Ellie.

"One hundred and sixty."

The officer looked her in the eye and said, "That's amazing."

It stunned Ellie to receive the dignity and respect she actually deserved. When the woman stamped her papers—approved!—she kept her euphoria bottled up, lest the officer wonder why she was *that* excited to leave Tanzania. In October 2018, Ellie flew to New York City, and the night before our She's the First event, which she was slated to keynote, we had a surprise for her.

Michelle Obama was in town, and she wanted to speak with a group of young women from around the world, to hear about the challenges they'd overcome—in other words, their resilience and grit. The Obama Foundation had saved a seat for Ellie, right next to Mrs. Obama.

For two hours, Ellie took part in the discussion and told Mrs. Obama the same story you just read, about her election loss and its longer-term victory for another woman. Ellie's story made such an impression on Mrs. Obama that the former first lady shared it to her Instagram page, celebrating Ellie for the remarkable changemaker she is. Can you imagine what Ellie's life would be like today had her visa not been granted? She wouldn't have the support of the world's most admired woman and, with it, the ability to inspire girls back home in her community that anything is possible. In Ellie's words:

So many emotions overcame me as I reflected on where I had come from, as the last born of nine, never knowing what the world had in store for me. When I was growing up, my brothers told me that I was the future wife of another man and I should be married. Instead, I was the girl who pushed, who was stubborn, as my brothers claimed, who wanted to do the things my brothers did—including getting an education.

What about my brothers now? After I met Michelle Obama, they saw me as a role model and sent their own daughters to school.

Some people simply do not understand why we care and invest so much of ourselves in girls' education. I wake up every day knowing that Michelle has put her faith in me, and I have a very huge responsibility to reach out to as many communities as possible to make sure that more girls have the necessary support and materials to stay in school. This dream is what gets me out of bed every day. I will never stop until girls' rights and education are something for which we no longer have to fight.

We know what we're fighting against, and we do use that knowledge to fire us up and motivate us in our work. But this story reminds us what we fight *for*. Find what you fight for and hold it tight; you might see it's one way to build your resilience to be tough as a tardigrade.

chapter ten

DO SOMETHING
THAT MATTERS

WE STARTED THIS book by considering your dash, the dash that separates the date you were born from the date that, well, you're destined to die. *What will your dash mean?* Kudos to you for having the courage to do some digging and seek an answer. By this point, we hope that tiny little punctuation mark has galvanized you, bringing even more energy to your life and how you live it.

Your dash will likely hover, quietly and almost forgotten, in the backdrop of your everyday life. It's not something you think about every waking moment. We don't. Other questions are more overpowering. For us, day to day, we wonder: Why is the life of a child in the United States valued more than that of a child somewhere in Uganda or Guatemala or India? Or, why is the life of a white woman in New York or Atlanta or anywhere more valuable than that of a Black or Latinx woman? (Just look at maternal mortality rates: Black women die of pregnancy-related causes at a rate that is *three times* higher than that of white women. Most pregnancy-related deaths are preventable.) That kind of inequity fires us up.

Every once in a while, a loss happens that forces us to think deeply about that little dash, the one that is still beautifully open-ended for you. For us, that happened six years into doing the work of She's the First. In 2015, we faced an unimaginable loss.

We mentioned earlier that She's the First has more than 225 campus chapters across the globe, including in the United States, India, Singapore, Ghana, Australia, and the United Kingdom. The students who organize events and fundraisers and advocate for girls' rights bring us enormous pride.

The first chapter was at Syracuse University, when Christen was a student, and the second was at the University of Notre Dame in Indiana. Neither of us had been to Indiana at that point, but like all social movements, word of mouth travels faster and more broadly than you ever will. Monica Townsend, a student at Notre Dame, had heard about STF through her cousin Rachel, Tammy's best friend, and she started a chapter. A few years later, Monica's younger sister Victoria went off to Dartmouth College and started a chapter of her own.

In the Townsend family, there were three daughters, and, later, the youngest sister, Rebecca, wanted to follow in Monica's and Victoria's footsteps. She asked if she could start a chapter at her high school. At the time, our campus chapters were only at colleges and universities, but Rebecca begged us for permission to be the first and we thought, well, if she's anything like Monica and Victoria, then surely she can do this, too. And thus, our first high school campus chapter was born at Immaculate High School in Danbury, Connecticut, with Rebecca as the founding president. Under Rebecca's leadership, the chapter organized many creative advocacy and fundraising events, including a Zumbathon and "dress-down day" fundraiser. She was constantly pushing her traditional, uniform-wearing Catholic high school to approve all sorts of first-time events in the name of building excitement for the mission.

After Rebecca graduated, she had her sights set on the University of Notre Dame, where she'd work her way up the ranks to take over the chapter her sister had founded. She loved STF so much that she couldn't wait for the new school year to begin and to take on new projects for girls' rights at the university level. In June, she enthusiastically emailed STF to ask if she could help out in the office over the summer. It was the last time we would hear from her.

Two weeks later, on the Fourth of July holiday weekend, Tammy got an early morning call while waiting for a bus. The sky was already a cotton candy blue; it looked like the kind of day where nothing could go wrong. When her best friend's name popped up on the screen, Tammy was surprised—it was even earlier out West where she lived. Rachel, recently married, must be calling with some good news. *Did she get a new job? Was she pregnant?*

In an instant, Tammy realized how wrong she was. Rachel's voice cracked on the phone. Rebecca had been struck by a car the night before while out with friends to see the fireworks. "She didn't make it," Rachel whispered. Tammy tried to make sense of what she was hearing: *How was all of New York City still buzzing around her when the world just wasn't making any sense?*

The first person Tammy texted was Christen. A few days later, with our colleague Katie, who ran the campus program, we attended Rebecca's funeral in Connecticut. The three of us sat stunned and saddened like everyone there. But we were also overwhelmed as donations to She's the First started appearing in Rebecca's honor. People kept talking about her passion in championing the cause. It was her legacy. She's the First was not supposed to be a seventeen-year-old's legacy—it was supposed to be her extracurricular activity—but in Rebecca's short life, that's what it became. With funds Rebecca had raised and money later donated in her memory, the community fully funded the complete education of a young Ugandan girl, aptly named Joy, through her high school graduation.

At the funeral, Rebecca's sisters, Monica and Victoria, eulogized her by sharing how they had been sitting in Rebecca's bedroom, on her bed, as they tried to process their living nightmare. Under Rebecca's pillow, they found a piece of paper folded up. On the outside: "To the future Rebecca Townsend." Inside, it was a letter Rebecca had written as a high school sophomore for a class assignment. The teachers had just recently returned the letters to Rebecca and the other graduating seniors.

In it, she wrote three wishes she had, two of which came true while she was in high school:

1. Kiss in the rain
2. Fly to Spain

Tragically, she achieved the third wish with her death:

3. Save a life

The sudden moment when the vehicle swerved at them, Rebecca pushed one of her friends out of the way, saving his life. This story would later go viral. Rebecca's older sister Victoria created a #RememberingRebecca hashtag on social media to memorialize her sister with acts of kindness. To this day, we have never forgotten Rebecca's dedication to She's the First. Funds that were and continue to be raised in her memory have educated girls in Uganda and beyond, leaving a lasting impact on families and communities around the world.

WE DON'T WANT YOU TO FORGET what brought you to this book in the first place, no matter what happens next. Rebecca inspires us every day, but whoever your personal inspirations are, you made it this far and now have all the essential tools you need to charge ahead.

We wish we could wrap up your Impact Plan journey as we did with our fellows in Guatemala, in the open air, surrounded by fragrant blossoms, as each one stood up and talked about her goals: "I want to _____ because I believe that _____. Therefore, my project is _____. And I will have success when _____."

When you look back at your Impact Plan, you will see you now have all you need to do this as well. Pick out one of your most exciting goals and just say it out loud. "I want to offer time on the weekend [resource!] to a nonprofit helping refugees [partnership!] because I believe that everyone deserves a safe community [North Star!]. Therefore, my goal is to mentor a family [action!]. And I will have success when I have helped that family reach their goals for their first few years of resettlement in my community [accountability!]." If you were part of our fellowship, overcoming your nerves to speak your intention in front of your peer group, you'd get raucous applause right about now. You'd deserve it. Because even though the road from here is a long one (and that would be a fortunate thing), you have what you didn't on page one: direction, clarity, and focus.

Remember Stephanie, who was in our very first group of Impact Planners—the one who decorated her bedroom wall with colorful Post-its? She later told us that creating an Impact Plan changed the way she approaches the rest of her life. "Prior to this training, I battled with impostor syndrome and would often take on responsibilities and activities that I thought would earn me this impossible perfection award. I have learned that I do not have the bandwidth for every cause that lights a fire under me." Instead, Stephanie asks herself, *What is my North Star?* when approaching the most meaningful decisions she has to make. "Thank you for being real, for opening my eyes to choices and helping me to shift from getting it all done to getting things done with purpose and factor in personal satisfaction when choosing."

Like other Impact Planners, Stephanie ultimately realized that in order to create the world she wants to live in, she had to align her values with her actions and be consistent with *fewer* commitments that supported one big outcome, versus taking on too much and stalling.

After a decade of cofoundership and twenty-odd years navigating the complexities of service, we found the secret to success really is quite simple:

Changing the world starts with changing your own life.

The most important order of business any Impact Advisor has is guiding you to see that improving the world doesn't have to be cryptic and inaccessible. It shouldn't be saccharine and oversimplified either. It is hard work to think outside yourself, to see the world through the perspective of others and as part of larger systems you can't control. That work of understanding your ripple effect on the world begins with *you*. How do you prioritize? Where do you put your most precious resources? Which biases are you choosing to question?

As we get ready to bid farewell (for now) and send you on your way, know that you can always come back to these pages and exercises for a refresher or an update to your Impact Plan. Life never stays the same—there will be many transitions, planned and unexpected. There will be difficult questions to consider and moral decisions to make. The one constant remains the tools you have at your disposal to pick them apart, weigh them, and build a path forward.

You're coming out of this book with an Impact Plan that will keep you grounded and honest with yourself, your goals, and your vision. Don't forget that this plan is a living document. Revise it for your changing needs and knowledge.

As you look back on your Impact Plan, recognize that:

- You showed discretion in aligning your actions with a North Star, an ultimate outcome for the change you most want to see, the justice you most want to bring to the world. You drew upon this North Star from personal experience and understand the limitations of your perspective—as well as the immense value.
- You allowed your mind to wander in the possibilities of what one could do before you judged yourself on their plausibility.
- You pulled out every last resource you could think of at your disposal right now and weighed them carefully to prioritize what you can give.
- You considered the components of an Impact Pitch, to reach out to groups you can partner with for collective impact, efficiently and effectively.

- You set goals by level of effort from high to easy across three key fields of play: the personal, political, and professional.
- You acknowledged your biases so that you can continue addressing them.
- You recognized Band-Aids for what they are as short-term solutions and explored the importance of Systems Solutions (and how to sidestep Misguided Moves).
- You refreshed your tactics for building a network that can support you, teach you, and keep you accountable.

As for the two of us, we have more to do at She's the First, scaling up our work with local partners so we can reach tens of thousands more girls. Neither of us knows for sure what the journey of supporting STF from the outside looks like yet, but our own Impact Plans will guide us. For the last three years, developing this process has given us the chance to serve our own North Stars, which point toward equity for women and girls, by giving others who share that outcome the tools to plug into the movements we value. And for all the readers with different North Stars, we hope our issues intersect with yours and our work can rise up together.

With the final words of this chapter, we are ever closer to evolving our High Effort goal of "Writing a book" into "Getting it into as many hands as possible" so that the words on these pages become a living, breathing conversation we can continue to engage in. Every High Effort goal traces back to the smallest steps. Ten years ago, the small effort to post a video to YouTube called "She's the First" added up to this. More than ten years ago, the even tinier effort of adding each other as Facebook friends and having a conversation about an issue of shared concern—girls' lack of access to education and the way girls are criticized for and hindered by getting pregnant—added up to this.

REBECCA'S SISTERS FOUND THE LETTER she had written to her future self as a high school sophomore. After Rebecca's passing, at She's the First, we found another letter she had written. She had addressed it to the future leader of the chapter she had started at her high school.

Once a year, campus chapter leaders come together for an annual summit that trains them to be more effective advocates for girls' rights and gender equality. It's a tradition for chapter presidents to write a letter to the future leader who will take their place. The following year, when that student attends the summit, they open their predecessor's letter.

Before we attended her funeral, we opened Rebecca's letter and brought it to her family. They have given us permission to share part of it here with you:

> *Always make the effort to make EVERYONE feel appreciated. All in all, be intentional with everything that you do. Leave a footprint for someone to follow in. When you're gone, how do you want to be remembered? I would say: Be remembered for something special. Do something that matters.*
>
> Love,
> Rebecca Townsend, President

We'll leave you with Rebecca's powerful words: **Do something that matters.**

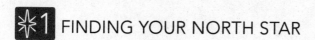

impact plan workbook

✳1 FINDING YOUR NORTH STAR

IMPACT IS PERSONAL

What circumstances or experiences define who you are and how you see the world?

List a few:

WHAT MOVES YOU?

If you open a news website right now, which stories stir emotions like anger, heartbreak, and hope? Is there a documentary you saw and never forgot? A nonfiction book that you couldn't keep to yourself and recommended to multiple people? An article that you posted to Facebook with a passionate caption? Note those here:

HOW DO YOU SPEND YOUR TIME?

What are the movements, community needs, or organizations that compel you to show up, be it in a rally, march, community service, family care, event, or volunteer or pro bono capacity? If you don't currently have any of these, list some places or causes you would be interested to explore.

LET'S TALK MONEY

When are you moved to donate? What kinds of causes or situations inspire you to give? List the last few places you've given money, even in small amounts. This might have been to causes, organizations, political campaigns, or neighborhood needs.

PULL IT TOGETHER

What are the connecting themes in the causes and stories that matter to you? Did you list any of the same issues multiple times in these exercises? Note those here:

_____   _____

_____   _____

_____   _____

NARRATIVE CONNECTIONS

When creating an Impact Plan, connecting your own narrative to the work you do will help you to have empathy, inspire others, *and* practice resilience. In the left-hand column below, list the issues you noted previously, and then drop key life experiences or circumstances on the right-hand side. Next, draw lines to connect the issues to your experiences.

Issues That Matter to Me   **Experiences That Have**
                                                          Affected Me

Take a look at the lines you've drawn. Wherever you're able to connect an issue that matters to you with an experience that affects or has affected you directly, this is the zone where you will find your North Star.

ENVISION THE FUTURE YOU WANT

Based on the lines you drew above, write the top issue area here:

Now, we'll envision how the world will have changed when the threats to this issue are finally gone.

> *You've just woken up, and it's twenty years in the future. You wake with a certainty that all is well in the world, that all is at peace. You know that as you progress through your day, you'll see examples of exactly that. So, you go outside into your neighborhood. What do you see there? Who do you talk to? What is different about the way you interact with people or the way they interact with each other? What is different about your surroundings? As you go to school or work, what seems different? When you turn on the news, what story is on?*

For full effect, close your eyes and let this scene play out like a movie in your head. Set your phone timer for three minutes and just see what shows on the screens of your eyelids. When you've finished, answer these questions:

What's a news headline in your future world that reflects the success of defeating the social problem you identified?

_____

_____

_____

What's the biggest change between the world we live in today and this version of the future?

_____

_____

YOUR NORTH STAR

In your Impact Plan, the North Star represents your end goal, the future you want to see.

Your North Star combines all of the previous exercises: your past experiences, your current interests, and your ideal future.

You should be able to visualize your North Star. Your expression of it should also do the following:

- Inspire you when you hear it
- Be personal to you
- Identify the *who*—who or what will be impacted?
- Be self-sustaining, not tasked to you or dependent on your actions. In other words, avoid the verb *help* (i.e., rather than "help immigrants have equal rights," "immigrants have equal rights"). If the problem is solved, what will happen?

Here are some examples to help you think through:

- Marginalized communities have strong mental health services
- Immigrants experience equal rights
- Justice for Indigenous communities
- Pregnancy and childbirth are safe for every mother
- The planet is protected for future generations
- People with disabilities are represented as strong and valued
- Girls have high self-esteem
- The elderly are cared for with dignity
- Gender equality exists in the workplace
- My government thrives on diverse (gender, race, class) representation
- No one lives in fear of gun violence
- Kids in my community are healthy and educated
- Everyone in my community has a home
- All kids can explore their imagination and enjoy the arts
- Animals are treated with respect and kindness
- Extreme poverty no longer exists

Fill in this statement with words that feel right in your gut:

My ideal world is one where

_____

That is your North Star.

✳2 POSSIBILITIES BEFORE PLAUSIBILITY

Take fifteen minutes to brainstorm any conceivable way in which a person could create impact for your North Star. Remember: Don't get caught up on the plausibility of the ideas. You're imagining what *any* person could do to push toward that North Star, not judging whether that should be you. By the time you're finished, you should have a list of ideas that encompasses the small, everyday actions, all the way up to some big, audacious ones.

RESOURCE INVENTORY

List resources that you can offer to an organization, movement, or group aligned with your North Star. We've included examples to get you started.

Assets (for example, a car, space to host an event, equipment to be shared)	**Network** (for example, connections to people who can give their resources, groups of people who would host an event)	**Skills** (for example, graphic design, photography, event coordination, engineering, languages)
Time (quantify it—free weekends, ten hours per month, one month per year)	**Money** (how much could you reasonably give per month or per year?)	**Experience** (for example, personal story to be shared with mentees or published, advising on a program or project)

From this list, circle three or four resources you'd like to put to use in your Impact Plan.

THE SEESAW TEST

If you're struggling to narrow your top resources down to three or four, try this doodling exercise. Write down two of your top resources across from each other and then picture a seesaw between them. Which resource do you have more of? Whether it's because you have a higher availability in that area or because you're simply more excited about it than the other, imagine that the more bountiful resource is the heavier one. Slant a line between the resources as a seesaw would land.

In the example below, the Impact Planner was debating whether to give $25 each month or to engage her women's group at work in fund-raising. Ultimately, she realized she needed to do more groundwork to get her women's group ready to host events, so for now, she feels more able to give funds than to utilize her network.

Women's group at work  **$25 a month**

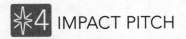 IMPACT PITCH

Review your answers to earlier exercises and respond to the following questions:

What is your North Star?

Why is this issue important to you?

What are the top three skills you want to offer?

Why are you qualified to offer those particular skills?

What are other resources you want to offer?

Now you have a snapshot of what you can give to an existing cause or organization. When reaching out, you can use this pitch template:

Thank you for all you do to work toward a world where [your North Star]. This issue is so important to me because [personal experience/reason]. By day, I am a [insert qualifications] and you can read more about me on my LinkedIn page: [link].

I'd like to find a way to be part of what you do. I appreciate that you are busy and likely have many offers of help, so to provide some guidance around where I could be the most useful, I wanted to be up front about what I can possibly provide:

[List a few skills or resources]

I can commit to about [time] per [frequency]. I'm available [specify mornings, weekends, evenings, etc.], and the ideal project for me is [ongoing/short-term, etc.].

Please let me know if and how I could match with your needs.

Successful matches will become commitments on your Impact Plan!

✳5 IMPACT AT WORK

To assess whether your job aligns with your long-term impact goals, we recommend asking yourself these questions. Use your Impact Journal for more space.

What are the values and impact of the company I currently work for?

_____

☐ I am okay with this   ☐ I am so not okay with this

What are the policies in place at my workplace?

_____

☐ I am okay with this   ☐ I am so not okay with this

What are the values and policies I'd want to see in place, to align with my North Star?

_____

☐ I think I could contribute   ☐ I don't think this change is
   to this change   feasible

If you decided your work aligns with your goals, great! Carry on. If you think you can create change in your workplace, write down a few ideas you have here. This might include starting a union, changing your clientele, or pushing for better policies.

_____

_____

_____

If you don't think change is feasible and it is important to you that your work matches your North Star, keep a lookout for new opportunities that *do* align.

✳6 PULL IT TOGETHER

You made it! To create your Impact Plan (on page 198), you'll bring together the exercises you've completed.

The first thing you want to do is **ink your North Star at the top**. This is ultimately your through line. Though your plan may change over time, your North Star is likely to stay fairly consistent throughout your life.

EVERYDAY IMPACT POINTS (6–8)

Once you've got your North Star down, turn your attention to the bottom of your page, where you will fill in your Easy Effort actions. Here's how to decide on your Everyday Impact Points:

> Is it something you can do on a regular basis without expending too much energy?
>
> Can you easily afford it?
>
> Can you make it a habit or a recurring action?
>
> Does it fit easily into your life as it exists now, without adjusting too much?
>
> Does it align with your North Star?

MEDIUM EFFORT ACTIONS (3–4)

These commitments take up more scheduled time and belong in the center of your Impact Plan. Here's how to identify them:

> Is this an action that requires you to spend slightly more time, energy, funds, or resources than you normally would?
>
> Is this something that is an ongoing project or volunteer role?
>
> Can you stretch yourself a little to achieve this?
>
> Does it align with your North Star?

HIGH EFFORT ACTIONS (1–3)

There is a reason this box is the smallest on the Impact Plan. Ask yourself:

> Is this a big, audacious goal?
>
> Is this something you would feel immensely proud to accomplish?
>
> Does it require you to really stretch yourself and to grow along the way?
>
> Does it impact your North Star in a significant way?

impact plan

your north star

high effort

||||

||||

||||

medium effort

☐☐

☐☐

☐☐

☐☐

easy effort

☐☐   ☐☐

☐☐   ☐☐

☐☐   ☐☐

☐☐   ☐☐

SAMPLE IMPACT PLAN

---

your north star

A world where everyone has their basic needs met and feels safe

---

high effort

HHH *Become foster/adoption certified and work toward adoption within 5 years*

HHH *Finish my M.S. in Nonprofit Management while web-design freelancing for start-ups, to sharpen my skills and eventually translate them into a full-time role in social good*

HHH *Set aside $1,000 a year to distribute to campaigns from selected organizations*

---

medium effort

☐☐ *Donate 12 hours of pro bono web design a month on Taproot+ or Catchafire*

☐☐ *Dedicate 6 Saturdays a year to volunteering at North Brooklyn Angels*

☐☐ *Volunteer at one New Sanctuary Coalition accompaniment per month*

☐☐ *Commit to my own care by regularly attending therapy, meeting with my church group, and/or taking dance classes*

---

easy effort

☐☐ *Vote in every election*

☐☐ *Carry snacks to offer on my subway commute to those in need*

☐☐ *To best of my ability, buy goods/gifts from businesses with fair labor practices*

☐☐ *Write a monthly note of affirmation to a friend, mentor, government official, or personal hero*

☐☐ *Make small monthly donations to my top 3 nonprofits*

☐☐ *Compost all eligible food waste*

☐☐ *Send a weekly postcard or call an elected rep to advocate for fair housing, immigration reform, etc.*

✳7 YOUR IMPACT LIST

As you review your social media lists, newsletter inbox folder, podcast player, and personal relationships, jot down the names of experts, leaders, and firsthand advocates you value and want to keep close.

EXPERTS	LEADERS	FIRSTHAND ADVOCATES
1.	1.	1.
2.	2.	2.
3.	3.	3.
4.	4.	4.
5.	5.	5.
6.	6.	6.
7.	7.	7.
8.	8.	8.
9.	9.	9.
10.	10.	10.

Do a quick scan of these names and double-check:

1. Do you see different races, genders, generations, classes, geographic areas represented?
2. Is there a mix of perspectives from the nonprofit sector, politics, activism, and academics?
3. Which categories of potential advisory board members (personal connections, experts, or leaders) seem homogenous and could be more diverse?

It looks like you've got yourself an Impact Advisory Board!

✳8 PROGRESS LOG

What wins did you and the purposeful groups you contribute to experience lately? Keep a running list on a separate page of your Impact Journal. On the days you face a setback and feel discouraged or insignificant, come back to this proof of your progress. You'll be glad you have it!

My Wins	Collective Wins

YOU'RE READY TO TAKE ON THE WORLD

... or at least, your own part in it! Your Impact Plan and what you've done to ensure it's full of Systems Solutions, informed by experts, and supported by your network is proof that you've put in the work. Now? Put it into action. You can always come back to your Impact Plan and revise it along the way; don't forget that this is a living document, one that should fit into your life. Tape your Impact Plan where you'll often see it and get started—the world is waiting for you. You are a changemaker.

Tell us how it went and find more advice for your journey at planyourimpact.com.

ACKNOWLEDGMENTS

First and foremost, our gratitude to the She's the First community is limitless. To our talented staff, dedicated board of directors, passionate campus chapters, inspiring partner organizations, and most of all, the unstoppable girls we serve: You give us every reason to wake up and work each day. And to the girls who've grown into women whom we're proud to call our friends, thank you for trusting us. Ellie, it is always an honor to share your story; thank you for letting us tell it here.

Writing a book is one of the hardest projects we've ever done. We are beyond grateful to the literary team who made it possible: our agent, Kathy Schneider, for spotting our potential early on and steering our proposal in the right direction; our whip-smart executive editor, Colleen Lawrie, for taking it to the next level, and all of PublicAffairs for giving *Impact* a home. It takes a village (Kaitlin Carruthers-Busser, Miguel Cervantes, Lindsay Fradkoff, Christina Palaia, and Brooke Parsons, among others) and our work is better because of you.

Kathy Treat, thank you for believing in us from the very first step, for loving the people behind the work, and for bringing the brilliant Jennifer Grant into our lives. Jen, thank you for helping us snap out of our self-doubts and organize our thoughts.

Thanks to the women who joined our original Impact Plan pilots at The Wing and over Google Hangouts . . . your trust in us made this entire journey possible.

Thanks to Shaunice Hawkins, Katie Riley, Lili Siegel, Jacquelyn Simone, and Jessica Watson for working with us to ensure these pages were welcoming to all. Lauren Smith Brody, Harriet Brown, Annie Ellman, Margo Gladys, Rachel Hofstetter, Andrea Lontoc, Susan McPherson, Erin Leigh Patterson, Perrie Rizzo, Gemma Rogers, Katie Sanders, Hart Seely, Ann Shoket, Kate White, and Leslie Zaikis: thanks for going the extra mile with your honesty, wisdom, and encouragement throughout this process. Derek Li, thank you for helping us design our Impact Plan. Claire and Jennie, thanks for toasting to this book at the very beginning. Thank you to the Townsend family for giving us your blessing to end with Rebecca's unforgettable words.

FROM CHRISTEN

Evan, thank you for showering me with the most important things in life: blankets, food, patience, and love. Your light has changed the way I look at the world, and life is better with you in it. Gma and Mom, thank you for raising me to be who I am today, and for loving me fiercely no matter what. Kevin, being your big sister has been one of life's greatest gifts—thank you for putting up with me. Chrissy, thank you for being the best father a girl could ask for; Sue, for being my ally in text threads and dinner conversations; Kathi, for your generous heart; Emily, for your old soul and thoughtful ways. Paul and Trish, thank you for the generous use of your fireplace and for welcoming me into your family.

Thank you to my many English teachers and writing professors over the years, from North Pocono to Syracuse University, for encouraging me every step of the way. To Mahesh, Angelica, Deepa, Cynthia, Yassin, Travis, and Vilma: The impact you're creating in the world continually inspires me to work harder and better. Thank you for making the world better for girls everywhere, for your wisdom and your leadership. Steph, Molly, Kate, Megan, Carly, Kat, Brian, Hatz, Sara, Philippe, Julie, Michelle, Britt: Your wine nights, phone calls, and encouragement give me the courage to say yes to so much, including writing this— thank you for being there.

And finally, to my work wife, Tammy: Thank you for saying yes to that hummus date all those years ago. There's no one I'd rather walk alongside as a leader—or an author!

FROM TAMMY

My deepest thanks go to the two people who've supported me the longest and worked the hardest to set me up for success in life: my mom, Cheryl, and dad, Scott. Without you, I wouldn't have experienced so many "firsts." Thank you for your unconditional love and for never doubting my dreams. Shelley, thank you for your thoughtfulness; it makes me happy that my earliest memories of books include you. To my late Grandma, Pop Pop, Grammie, and Grampie, whose love shaped my childhood: I feel you smiling down on me!

Michael: You're my favorite person in the universe for a reason. Thank you for being my number 1 cheerleader. Turns out you're an exceptional editor, too! You (and Wally) bring me endless joy and cuddles. You gave me the love, laughs, space, and breaks I needed on the busy weekends when this book came to be. You're my half orange and I love you with my whole heart.

To every friend and mentor who checked in to ask how the book was going, who provided feedback, who commented on Instagram updates, who contributed to STF over the years: It made all the difference. Thank you.

I'm forever appreciative to South Brunswick High School, the South Brunswick Public Library, The College of New Jersey, and New York Women in Communications for influencing my journey as a writer and reader.

And to the world's best cofounder, Christen: from DC to T&C, I'd go anywhere to dream up plans with you! We've come so far, and creating impact with you has been the adventure of a lifetime.

NOTES

INTRODUCTION

Stat, Terri Yablonsky. "Be Generous: It's a Simple Way to Stay Healthier." *Chicago Tribune*, August 6, 2015. http://www.chicagotribune.com/lifestyles/health/sc-hlth
-0812-joy-of-giving-20150806-story.html.

CHAPTER ONE

Remen, Rachel Naomi. "Helping, Fixing, or Serving?" Lion's Roar, August 6, 2017.
https://www.lionsroar.com/helping-fixing-or-serving.

CHAPTER TWO

DoSomething.org. "11 Facts About Global Poverty," accessed March 29, 2020. https://
www.dosomething.org/us/facts/11-facts-about-global-poverty#fn1.

Financial Samurai. "The Average Percent of Income Donated to Charity Can Improve," accessed March 29, 2020. https://www.financialsamurai.com/the-average
-percent-of-income-donated-to-charity.

Kenny, Charles. "We're All the 1 Percent." The Optimist (blog), Foreign Policy, February
27, 2012. https://foreignpolicy.com/2012/02/27/were-all-the-1-percent.

CHAPTER THREE

Confino, Jo. "Sustainable Corporations Perform Better Financially, Report Finds."
The Guardian, September 23, 2014. https://www.theguardian.com/sustainable
-business/2014/sep/23/business-companies-profit-cdp-report-climate-change
-sustainability.

Houser, Kristin. "How Many People Do You Need to Change the World?" World
Economic Forum, June 12, 2018. https://www.weforum.org/agenda/2018/06
/want-to-change-society-s-views-here-s-how-many-people-you-ll-need-on-your-side.

Talk of the Nation, NPR. "A Case For Cash Donations, Instead of Cans," November
2011. https://www.npr.org/2011/11/22/142661882/a-case-for-cash-donations
-instead-of-cans.

RECOMMENDED READS

Buchanan, Phil. *Giving Done Right* (New York: PublicAffairs, 2019).
Giridharadas, Anand. *Winners Take All* (New York: Alfred A. Knopf, 2018).
Oluo, Ijeoma. *So You Want to Talk About Race* (New York: Basic Books, 2019).
Saad, Layla F. *Me and White Supremacy* (Naperville, IL: Sourcebooks, 2020).

CHAPTER FOUR

Herman, Todd. "The Field of Play." Alter Ego Effect, February 5, 2019. https://alterego
   effect.com/extras.
Matthews, Gail. "Goals Research Summary." Dominican University of California.
   https://www.dominican.edu/sites/default/files/2020-02/gailmatthews-harvard
   -goals-researchsummary.pdf.
Waxman, Olivia B. "The Inspiring Depression-Era Story of How the 'March of Dimes'
   Got Its Name." *Time*, January 3, 2019. https://time.com/5062520/march-of
   -dimes-history.

CHAPTER FIVE

Allardice, Lisa. "Chimamanda Ngozi Adichie: 'This Could Be the Beginning of a Revo-
   lution.'" *The Guardian*, April 28, 2018. https://www.theguardian.com/books/2018
   /apr/28/chimamanda-ngozi-adichie-feminism-racism-sexism-gender-metoo.

RECOMMENDED READ

Eberhardt, Jennifer. *Biased* (New York: Penguin, 2019).

CHAPTER SIX

Contie, Vicki. "Brain Imaging Reveals Joys of Giving." NIH Research Matters, National Institutes of Health, US Department of Health & Human Services, June
   22, 2007. https://www.nih.gov/news-events/nih-research-matters/brain-imaging
   -reveals-joys-giving.
Kane, Becky. "Can't Work Towards Your Long-Term Goal? Blame Your Brain." *Fast
   Company*, November 29, 2018. https://www.fastcompany.com/90273724/cant
   -work-towards-your-long-term-goal-blame-your-brain.
Kindelan, Katie. "Donating Vacation Time to New Moms Is a Trendy Co-worker Baby
   Shower Gift." *Good Morning America*, July 18, 2018. https://www.goodmorning
   america.com/living/story/donating-vacation-time-moms-trendy-worker-baby
   -shower-55632450.
Martinez, Gina. "GoFundMe CEO: One-Third of Site's Donations Are to
   Cover Medical Costs." *Time*, January 30, 2019. https://time.com/5516037
   /gofundme-medical-bills-one-third-ceo.

CHAPTER SEVEN

Clarke, Chris. "6 Reasons That Floating Ocean Plastic Cleanup Gizmo Is a Horrible Idea." Redefine, KCET, June 4, 2015. https://www.kcet.org/redefine/6-reasons-that -floating-ocean-plastic-cleanup-gizmo-is-a-horrible-idea.

Gabrielle, Vincent. "A Crowdfunded Idea to Clean the Great Pacific Garbage Patch Is Now a $35-Million Nonprofit. Scientists Still Don't Think It'll Work." *Gizmodo*, February 8, 2019. https://earther.gizmodo.com/a-kickstarter-idea-to-clean -the-great-pacific-garbage-p-1832459898.

Martini, Kim. "The Ocean Cleanup, Part 2: Technical Review of the Feasibility Study." *Deep Sea News*, July 14, 2014. http://www.deepseanews.com/2014/07/the-ocean -cleanup-part-2-technical-review-of-the-feasibility-study.

INDEX

Credit: Gaby Deimeke

As founders of She's the First (STF), Christen Brandt and Tammy Tibbetts built a wildly successful girls' rights organization from the ground up, while helping others to unlock their impact potential. Christen and Tammy's work is supported by Michelle Obama's Girls Opportunity Alliance, the United Nations, Diane von Furstenberg, many major brands, more than two hundred campus chapters, and hundreds of thousands of everyday changemakers worldwide. They each live with their partners in Brooklyn, where you can find them meeting in the park to brainstorm on their latest ideas.

PublicAffairs is a publishing house founded in 1997. It is a tribute to the standards, values, and flair of three persons who have served as mentors to countless reporters, writers, editors, and book people of all kinds, including me.

I. F. STONE, proprietor of *I. F. Stone's Weekly*, combined a commitment to the First Amendment with entrepreneurial zeal and reporting skill and became one of the great independent journalists in American history. At the age of eighty, Izzy published *The Trial of Socrates*, which was a national bestseller. He wrote the book after he taught himself ancient Greek.

BENJAMIN C. BRADLEE was for nearly thirty years the charismatic editorial leader of *The Washington Post*. It was Ben who gave the *Post* the range and courage to pursue such historic issues as Watergate. He supported his reporters with a tenacity that made them fearless and it is no accident that so many became authors of influential, best-selling books.

ROBERT L. BERNSTEIN, the chief executive of Random House for more than a quarter century, guided one of the nation's premier publishing houses. Bob was personally responsible for many books of political dissent and argument that challenged tyranny around the globe. He is also the founder and longtime chair of Human Rights Watch, one of the most respected human rights organizations in the world.

·　　·　　·

For fifty years, the banner of Public Affairs Press was carried by its owner Morris B. Schnapper, who published Gandhi, Nasser, Toynbee, Truman, and about 1,500 other authors. In 1983, Schnapper was described by *The Washington Post* as "a redoubtable gadfly." His legacy will endure in the books to come.

Peter Osnos, *Founder*